Family Fables

How to Write and Publish Your Family's Story

Family Fables

How to Write and Publish Your Family's Story

Maisie Robson

Eynsford Hill Press

© Maisie Robson, 2006

Typeset and published by
Eynsford Hill Press
14 New Street
Wombwell
Barnsley
South Yorkshire
S73 0AE
United Kingdom

ISBNs 0 9542318 2 1
978 0 9542318 2 8

British Library Cataloguing in Publication Data
A catalogue record for this book is available from
the British Library.

Printed and bound in Great Britain
by Cromwell Press, Trowbridge, Wiltshire

CONTENTS

Chapter 1: Introduction

The Family History habit

In recent years there has been an explosion of interest in genealogy. *Family Tree Magazine* gets fatter with every issue and many similar titles have been launched. Perhaps the geographical dispersion of living relatives leaves us all with a need to find somewhere we belong. Rapid social change and the waning of religious belief may also be factors. Whatever the cause, family history research is now the third most popular hobby in the UK and the second most common reason for logging on to the internet. The BBC has broadcast popular television programmes on genealogy – 'The People Detective' and 'Who do you think you are?' – and the associated web site for 'Who do you think you are?' achieved 2½ million hits in the first two days.

The Boxes in the Attic

Since you have chosen to read this book, it's likely that you have already done a fair bit of 'sleuthing' and are sitting on files and boxes of undigested material. Buried in those files is a wealth of human interest stories that most writers would envy. Your family history research has also trained you in abstract thinking and the ability to evaluate and organise facts. You are therefore perfectly placed for the task of turning your raw research into a book. For most genealogists, going *back* into the past also involves going *sideways* into local and cultural history. Almost without knowing it, you have taught yourself a great deal of social history which would make an interesting background to the story of your ancestors' lives and struggles.

Researching the history of your family involved exploring history backwards. Now that you have decided to turn it into a book, you will find yourself inverting another usual procedure: authors typically get an idea for a book, *then* do the research. Family historians, by contrast, already have the research at their finger-tips. It simply needs organising. The chapters that follow offer common sense techniques for sorting your data and shaping it into a gripping story that could be published in book form. Three benefits arise from this:

❑ A book preserves your research in a compact and accessible form that will be treasured (not dreaded!) by your descendants.

❑ Your family's story could have commercial appeal. Think of the success of Frank McCourt's *Angela's Ashes* and Laurie Lee's *Cider With Rosie*.

❑ Your book will make a contribution to social history, smoothing the way for historians who follow after you.

There is another less tangible benefit. Creative writing is therapeutic for the writer – which perhaps explains why creative writing courses have in recent years become as popular as family history itself. By reading this book, you will learn to use words powerfully and imaginatively. Even if you finally decide that producing a full-length book about your family is too great a task, *Family Fables* includes writing ideas and exercises that are fun to attempt and will help you explore your potential as a writer. All writing is self-discovery. Charles Dickens described the process of writing as 'confidential interviews with myself'. Your antecedents deserve to be understood – and so do you.

Bringing the past back to life

Your research findings need to be shaped, and this means more than simply stringing facts together in chronological order. All too often, family history projects get stuck at the 'miscellaneous facts' stage – papers and pictures collected into boxes, loosely arranged in date order but lacking the narrative drive necessary for a publishable book. The next stage is to turn the odd documents and awkward data into a powerful page-turner.

Fiction and Non-Fiction

It's important to recognise that there are both literal truths and symbolic truths. This is the difference between the surface appearance and deeper reality. Having trained yourself as a researcher, you're now taking on the role of story-teller, mediating and interpreting the facts you have uncovered, giving them depth, meaning and resonance. Reality is constituted not just of facts but of subjective interpretation of facts. It could even be said that there is no history as such but just competing *histories*.

This not a new idea. The terms 'history' and 'story' were used interchangeably until the sixteenth century, and both derive from the same Latin word, *historia*. Over the last quarter-century, the boundaries between fiction and non-fiction have again become fluid and permeable. Novelists are turning to historical events for their subject matter and prize-winning biographers, autobiographers and even historians have wholeheartedly adopted the creative techniques of novelists.

There is nothing dishonest in imaginatively recreating your ancestors' lives: you simply need to be clear about what you are doing and ensure that your readers are not misled. Having studied and thought about your ancestors for so long, you should be able to put yourself in their shoes and imagine how they would react in various circumstances.

For the convenience of your readers, you could begin your book with a clarification. English professor David Lodge, for example, begins his biographical novel about Henry James (*Author, Author*) with a brief statement which includes the following:

Nearly everything that happens in this story is based on factual sources. With one insignificant exception, all the named characters were people. Quotations from their books, plays, articles, letters, journals, etc., are their own words. But I have used a novelist's licence in representing what they thought, felt, and said to each other.

Laurie Lee's shy note at the start of *Cider With Rosie* is even more relevant to those attempting autobiography: 'The book is a recollection of early boyhood, and some of the facts may be distorted by time.'

The popularity of 'faction' – the blend of fact and

fiction – is very good news indeed for family researchers. Bare data can be clothed with literary techniques and given thematic cohesion and drive. Chapter 2 outlines some developments in biography-writing which could be applied to your own project.

Becoming a writer

Anyone who has systematically explored their family history is more than capable of picking up the skills needed to write a book. Genealogists and local historians are capable researchers, comfortable with both secondary research (using books and the internet) and the primary research that involves visiting places and interviewing people. You now need to add imagination to your repertoire, entering into the lives of your ancestors, thinking and feeling as they did. Then by applying the common sense advice in chapter 10, you could take the next step and become not just a writer but a published author.

Many family historians are already computer literate and have a well-organised work-station in a spare bedroom or corner of the living room. There may also be computers in your local library which can be used free of charge on presentation of a library card. If you need help, ask the librarians about free courses or join the nearest Family History or Local History society, where there will be computer buffs among the membership eager to give you a helping hand. But you don't *need* a computer. Throughout history the vast bulk of books have been written with pen and paper. It is people, not gadgets, that write books and if you mean to be a writer, you will do it.

Whether you use a computer or not, your writing project will spawn a certain amount of loose paper and other paraphernalia. In the interests of domestic harmony and your own sanity, separate your writer's 'toolbox' from other family tasks. Keep all your writing materials together, on a separate table if possible, or in a cardboard box if need be. Include a clip-board so you can turn even casual furniture, or a car-seat, into a makeshift desk by writing on your knees. Prolific novelist Fay Weldon wrote some of her books sitting on the staircase, as this was the only quiet place in her house. Jot down ideas as soon as they occur to you, using pocket-sized scribble pads. Then write them up every evening – or once a week, if that rhythm suits you – on loose A4 lined paper, or use the computer if you have one. Exercise books are to be avoided as you don't know yet where each idea belongs. Loose sheets of paper in ring-binders are a much more flexible tool. You will inevitably experience false starts and find yourself going over the same ground, rewriting what you thought was finished. This is a normal part of a writer's life and is in no way a sign of failure. By keeping your work on loose sheets, the amount of rewriting is minimised.

Experiment with different writing schedules. We all have our different learning and writing styles and there is no right or wrong writing routine. But do please avoid the two most common diseases that afflict the would-be writer:

❑ Desk-drawer-itis: keeping notes in your desk drawer but never taking them out because there's always something more interesting, or easier, to do. Serious writers treat writing like a job and sit down to write whether they feel inspired or not.

❑ First-chapter-itis: endlessly tinkering with the first chapter as a way of avoiding getting on with the rest. I recommend that you produce a *complete* first draft, however rough and ready, before you do any revision. (Revision is covered in chapter 9.) A successful thriller writer has coined the slogan, 'Don't get it right, get it down'.

Writers' circles

Writing can be deeply fulfilling but it can also be lonely at times and there are days when it is all too easy to fall into apathy. Joining a writing class or writers' circle is a good move to overcome feelings of isolation. Many areas offer adult education classes on creative writing. These are run by qualified English teachers and students are encouraged to try different genres or types of writing – including poetry, which you may feel is not immediately relevant to you. A writers' circle on the other hand is an informal group, often held in someone's home or a corner of the library at little or no cost. If there isn't one in your town or village, ask around in your local Family History Society or Readers' Group in the library. Perhaps some of their members would, like you, enjoy meeting from time to time to discuss writing up their various projects.

Read broadly, make notes

If you enjoyed the research part of your family history project, don't worry – there is still more reading to be done! As a background to your writing project you should be reading biographies; social history books to provide useful facts and atmosphere; and creative writing books for tips on techniques. By evaluating biographies and family histories that are already published, as well as books on local and national history, you will be honing your critical powers and learning to revise and improve your own work. *Family Fables* draws attention to literary conventions and suggests how you can use them for your own purposes, or experiment with them for entirely new purposes; but it is vital to read widely, even indiscriminately. Even if a book really is bad, it is quite possible to get good ideas from bad books. Jot down in a notebook anything that makes you think.

Nothing is ever wasted. Everything that happens to you, every word you hear and read, even snatches of pop songs, can stimulate an idea for your own book. Writers are never 'off duty'. Other biographies, for example, can throw into relief how your family members differed from, or were similar to, people of the same period. Alternatively, the content of a particular biography may be irrelevant, but you can still learn from the biographer's literary style, the structure of the book, the layout and design.

Reading Fiction

Certain powerful themes recur in literature as plot devices (illness, an unhappy marriage, the death of a child) and you should study these to stimulate ideas for handling your own findings. Genres of literature have grown up around issues of lasting interest to human beings. Romance appeals to our need for affiliation, horror to our need to understand and control fear, regional sagas and rags-to-riches tales give meaning to lives constrained by poverty, and so forth. Family historians should ponder these to find the key to presenting their own research.

Picking up tips from the experts

Critically examining novels and creative non-fiction is one of the best ways to learn how a book is put together. Here is a quick exercise. Think of any novel or biography you admire and consider its different elements as if you were using it as a model to *teach* you how to write a book. The following prompt questions will help.

- ❑ Plot: what happens to the main characters? Are there any sub-plots?
- ❑ What conflict generates the action? Is the main character struggling against society, a set of individuals (e.g. the bosses) or his/her own personality? Are the characters searching for something?
- ❑ Is it a page-turner? Were you, the reader, kept wondering what's going to happen next?

- ❏ What period of time was needed for the story to unfold?
- ❏ Where was the story set?
- ❏ How were the characters introduced and described?
- ❏ What are the themes of the book?
- ❏ Is the author's language simple to understand or rather 'poetic'? Has the author chosen an appropriate style for the geographical region and historical period in which the story is set?
- ❏ Is it all written in the past tense or are there some episodes written in the present or future tenses?
- ❏ From whose point of view do we see the action?
- ❏ Is the story explained mainly through narrative summary or through dramatic scenes with lots of action and dialogue?

As an example, consider Jane Austen's handling of plot and character in *Pride and Prejudice.* The **plot** follows the progress of a romance between the proud Darcy and prejudiced Elizabeth. They fight against their own natures, their families and a wider society that does not consider Elizabeth a good enough match for someone as rich as Darcy. There are two **sub-plots:** the marriage-of-convenience of Elizabeth's friend Charlotte, and Elizabeth's silly teenage sister eloping with a soldier.

Jane Austen uses a wide variety of different techniques for introducing and developing **characters**: they appear in person, are described in the conversation of others, introduce themselves in letters they write, appear as characters in letters written by others, and so on.

Dialogue is the quickest way to convey a character's personality, and Austen uses this to devastating effect in showing up the vulgarity of some of the characters. Characters aren't always described fully when they first appear in the novel. The triviality of Elizabeth's teenage sisters is not fully revealed until two-thirds of the way through the novel, when Elizabeth has to share a coach home with them and their immature behaviour and conversation is painfully apparent.

Whether your own choice for this exercise was a novel or a biography, analysing it should have given you some insight into how the author structured the story – something a reader does not usually consider when engrossed in a book.

The next chapter contains an outline of biography as a genre and explains how to turn your family history into a 'group biography'. Then in chapter 3 you will begin to organise your own research material, ready to write it up as a book.

Chapter 2: Writing Biography

Throughout history, human beings have been insatiably curious about other human beings, so your family history research already has potential. Biographies are also a good place for a novice writer to start as the genre offers you a ready-made structure. At its simplest, the biographer gets the biographee from cradle to grave in the most interesting way possible. Yet there is still scope for you to organise the material you discover, recognising recurring patterns and themes. Not all facts are equal. Significance often lies in apparent trivia, and it is the biographer's privilege to identify the underlying shape of a life. Writing biography is a quest for meaning. Whereas biography used to be regarded as history's poor relation, it is now recognised as one of the creative arts.

Biography/Autobiography as a Genre

Expectations about the form and content of biographies and autobiographies have changed radically over the centuries.

The Dark Ages and Middle Ages saw the production of Lives of Saints which were highly idealised portraits written to induce religious fervour. They could boast little in the way of realistic characterisation.

In Elizabethan times there was a new interest in the individual and some biographies of political figures began to be written. A famous example is Thomas More's biography of Richard III which was published in 1513 and used by Shakespeare 80 years later as the basis for his play *Richard III*.

The first recognisable autobiographies were religious journals by Christian writers diligently recording their sins and bearing witness to the place of God in their daily lives. Most of these were not intended for publication, but John Bunyan, author of *Pilgrim's Progress,* did publish his *Grace Abounding to the Chief of Sinners* as an encouragement to other Christians. His purpose, therefore, was didactic … and some of the 'sins' he confesses to are very surprising!

In the eighteenth century, the standard biography consisted of the facts of the biographee's life rounded off with a conclusion that summed up their character. William Mason's biography of the poet Thomas Gray (author of 'Elegy Written in a Country Church-Yard') was an innovation. It consisted simply of Gray's letters with a linking commentary but no moralising. Mason wanted to let readers decide for themselves.

James Boswell's eighteenth-century classic *The Life of Samuel Johnson* (1791) went one step further. Boswell included not only Johnson's letters but transcripts of his conversations. Even more significantly, the biographer himself appears as a central character in the biography. Samuel Johnson himself was a noted biographer, and his technique was to include the 'domestic privacies … the minute details of daily life' which are very much a part of modern biography.

Boswell died in 1795 but he became, posthumously, the subject of an extraordinary paper-chase that brings home how arbitrary the survival of historical documents can be. Scholars believed that Boswell's own voluminous papers had been destroyed: the word 'buried' (i.e. in a mass of paper) had been wrongly printed as 'burned' in a key text about Boswell and would-be biographers took this at face value and stopped looking for material. Then in 1857 a Major Stone was shopping in France and found that a shopkeeper had wrapped some of his parcels in ancient letters signed 'James Boswell'. This started a century-long hunt for lost Boswelliana that was concluded only after the Second World War, quantities of material having been unearthed from different locations.

There is not always a happy ending, however. On the death of Charles Dickens in 1870, his friend John Forster undertook to write the first biography of this great English novelist. Unfortunately, Forster was old and ill and he soon tired of copying out Dickens' letters into his manuscript. Horrific as it now seems, Forster allowed himself the crude short-cut of scissors and paste bottle, cutting out the parts he wanted to quote, sticking them into his manuscript and throwing the mutilated letters away. He also destroyed his own manuscript as soon as the biography was printed. It has been estimated that 945 letters by Dickens were lost forever in this way, at what cost to scholarship one can only guess.

Modern biography was ushered in by a slim volume from Bloomsbury writer Lytton Strachey who reacted against the piety of many Victorian biographies. His *Eminent Victorians* appeared in the significant year of 1918, at the end of the war which brought to a close the cosy certainties of Victorian and Edwardian times. Strachey was deeply scornful of the bloated, family-authorised biographies of Victorian worthies and wrote witheringly of 'those two fat volumes … with their ill-digested masses of material, their slipshod style, their tone of tedious panegyric, their lamentable lack of selection, of detachment and design.'

Strachey's work has been characterised as an early foray into 'hostile biography'. His biographical victims (Florence Nightingale, Arnold of Rugby, Gordon of Khartoum and Cardinal Manning) are certainly given short shrift. Instead of assuming the posture of an acolyte kneeling in awed worship before the biographee, this biographer examines his subjects coldly from a great height and laughs at their weaknesses. His disdain is magnificent. Without Strachey, or someone very like him, we would not have seen the modern phenomenon of the muck-raking celebrity biography – those tawdry volumes that sell in their thousands by revealing or inventing sensational details of a celebrity's private life. Exquisite as *Eminent Victorians* is, Strachey opened a Pandora's box that is unlikely ever to be closed.

In the Victorian era and after, a market developed for biographies of famous novelists. Literary biography had become a lucrative industry and some writers were driven to desperate measures to protect their privacy. Determined to control his posthumous reputation, novelist Thomas Hardy secretly wrote his own biography and schemed to have it passed off after his death as the work of his second wife. The trickery was not discovered for twelve years.

Surviving relatives of deceased writers can present serious obstacles in the way of would-be biographers. The poet T S Eliot's widow denied biographer Peter Ackroyd permission to quote from even the published works of her late husband. Ackroyd however was undeterred, viewing the refusal as a challenge. His technique was to *refer to* persistent themes in Eliot's work (without quoting them: Mrs Eliot wouldn't let him) and allow the reader to make the connection to aspects of Eliot's life. The resulting biography is an heroic example of a biographer triumphing over seemingly impossible restrictions. As fellow biographer, Ian Hamilton, summed up: 'the unauthorised biographer had tracked down a great mass of accessible archive material and had managed to come up with a detailed, plausible and widow-proof account of Eliot's life.'

A very recent example of prize-winning literary biography is Jonathan Coe's account of the life of novelist B S Johnson, *Like A Fiery Elephant.* This innovative work is formally very interesting, including as it does (a) extracts from unpublished drafts of Johnson's novels, (b) verbatim remarks from interviewees (living witnesses), unmediated by any comment from the biographer, (c) numbered scenes and episodes from Johnson's life, and (d) numbered quotations from a selection of Johnson's letters. The overall impression is of raw data, as if Coe had presented the reader with notes for a biography, rather than a finished work. The reader takes a very active role in composing the story in his or her own mind. Since this was precisely what Johnson (the biographee) was aiming at with his experimental novels, Coe's chosen form is appropriate to the content. He has written an experimental biography of an experimental writer.

Since the turn of the last century and the passing away of those complacent Victorians, it has become painfully obvious that life is not always comprehensible and neat, that there are innumerable ways of looking at the same facts. This insight has had a profound effect on the novel, with techniques such as 'stream of consciousness' used to convey the multifariousness of human experience. As biography has developed as a genre, biographies and autobiographies are increasingly being written poetically, with material shaped according to theme and pattern rather than adhering rigidly to a chronological account. Gaps and contradictions can be tolerated because life is like that; moreover, readers like mysteries and many enjoy taking an active role in interpreting what they read. Biography is more and more seen not as a science but as an imaginative exercise.

Group biographies

Double or group biographies, such as the biography of a family, have become very popular. Family history projects are, in effect, longitudinal group biographies, so your project could well be in the vanguard of literary fashion.

Literary biographers such as Michael Holroyd and Richard Holmes have frequently taken on the challenge of writing about several people at once. This may be a group of friends, professional colleagues or indeed a family. Holmes has even claimed there is no such thing as the single-subject biography, as writing about *anyone* will necessarily involve a large supporting cast.

In his book about two eighteenth-century writers, *Dr Johnson and Mr Savage,* Holmes explores the perceptions of four men— the eponymous Johnson and Savage, James Boswell who wrote Johnson's biography, and Holmes himself. Holmes weighs all the evidence and concludes that all four are probably deluding themselves, misled by their emotions into misconstruing the facts. The life of Savage, Holmes states, is 'mysterious in the way it came to be told and reinterpreted, one version layering upon another, like a piece of complex geology'. Perhaps everyone's life is like that.

As early as 1907 Edmund Gosse wrote the 'double biography' *Father and Son* tracing the collapse of his relationship with his father Philip Gosse, zoologist and fundamentalist Christian. The resulting book is a wonderful joint portrait of two baffled men from the same family who seem to belong to different centuries. Their conflicts and mutual incomprehension are drawn with humour and compassion, making the book a lasting contribution to biography and literature alike. It bears some resemblance to Cecil Woodham-Smith's book about the Charge of the Light Brigade, *The Reason Why,* which attributes the fatal charge to animosity between Lord Lucan and Lord Cardigan. The focus of Woodham-Smith's volume is an exploration of the two men's characters and background: an example of biography being absolutely central to history.

More recently, Jonathan Raban's *Coasting* uses the structural device of a voyage — a trip round the coast of Great Britain in a tiny yacht — as the occasion for a meditation on his relationship with his parents. The journey, undertaken in the year of the Falklands conflict, enables Raban to physically revisit the scenes of his childhood and brood over family quarrels, a changing England and the effect that ageing has on personality. The best travel literature often includes autobiographical and confessional elements of this sort and would-be biographers can learn much from the genre.

The Ethics of writing Biography

Think back to all the family data you have collected. The information probably includes some family secrets, skeletons that your ancestors wanted kept firmly in the cupboard. All biographers are faced with difficult decisions about handling sensitive material, though what counts as 'sensitive' changes over the years, particularly where issues of a person's health, financial status and sexual habits are concerned. Until comparatively recently, it was a stigma to be born illegitimate; few people today would be distressed at such a fact being made public.

If some of your characters have living descendants, these surviving family members will often want you to write an idealised portrait of their deceased relatives. As a biographer you are dedicated to the truth, whether it is favourable or not. This involves you in a delicate balancing act – trying to maintain your integrity as a writer while keeping the family sufficiently happy to co-operate with you and trust you with access to documents and other information.

This dilemma is simplified for those writing either a work of 'Victorian' piety or an iconoclastic work designed to sweep away all pretence and expose the truth. In the former case, the family will be delighted to help you; in the latter, you probably shouldn't even ask them.

Since Victorian times, there has been a movement away from reticence, privacy and decorum in favour of disclosure, openness and the public's right to know. In days gone by, families would typically sift through posthumous papers and throw on a bonfire anything compromising about a deceased relative; today, they are more likely to deposit *all* the material in a public archive but place an embargo on the early release of certain papers. This solution protects both the feelings of the family in the present and the rights of scholars in the future, but is frustrating for a biographer who wants to get at the truth here and now. Chapter 9 suggests ways to cope with gaps in the evidence. Such mysteries and lacunae are by no means fatal to your book. In fact, some of the greatest biographies and autobiographies of the last century have been written with incomplete and contradictory evidence. Finding that some material is inaccessible can be a blessing in disguise

You the Biographer

The novelist Henry James wrote that life is inclusion and confusion while art is exclusion and selection. In your role as family historian, you seized everything you could find on the subject. However, some facts, interesting in their own right, won't deserve a place in the finished book, and you may have to relegate them to an Appendix or leave them out altogether. The writer's task is to get at the essence of the facts and, by juxtaposition and emphasis, reveal the *meaning* of a past life. You need to be able to read between the lines, making unusual connections to arrive at a symbolic truth.

You will by now be eager to make a start on your own 'group biography', so let's have a look at what's in those boxes of research.

Chapter 3: Organising your Material and Structuring your Book

What is your story about, and how can you best tell your story? You need to start sketching out your own answers to the questions:

- WHO: which ancestral line and which family members will your book be about?
- WHERE: where does the action take place?
- WHEN: what period of time will your book cover?
- WHAT and HOW: what happens? where is the conflict and tension?
- WHY: what overarching themes does your family story illustrate?

Your conclusions might look something like this:

- WHO: my branch of the Towser family, with particular reference to the Towser who entered the church in 1700 and his great-great-grandson who became a missionary in Polynesia.
- WHERE: focusing on the village of Carlton in the Fens but with excursions into other areas as family members sought jobs, fought wars and pursued crafts and professions further afield.
- WHEN: from earliest records to the Second World War.
- WHAT: highlighting the family members' progress as they struggled for (variously) survival, respectability, social and professional advancement, self-fulfilment and spiritual wholeness.

❑ HOW: how the Towsers achieved their goals in the teeth of poor health, prejudice, poverty and the stubborn social conditions into which they were born.
❑ WHY: the dreams and aspirations that motivated individual quests for satisfaction and achievement.

Have another look at your files or boxes of family history research. These will typically include a multiplicity of original documents (primary sources) some of which will ultimately prove more relevant than others. You might have collected and catalogued:

❑ family Bibles
❑ birth, baptism, death and marriage certificates
❑ photographs (with notes, perhaps, on who took them and why)
❑ newspaper clippings
❑ poor law records
❑ census returns
❑ parish registers
❑ diocesan records
❑ records of nonconformist denominations
❑ diaries, memoirs and letters
❑ manorial records
❑ transcripts of wills and inventories - giving valuable data on possessions and domestic interiors
❑ property records and maps
❑ tithe awards
❑ armed forces records - making an interesting link to *national* history

- ❑ police and court records
- ❑ immigration/emigration documents
- ❑ data on war graves and war memorials
- ❑ medical data about illness and diseases
- ❑ apprenticeship papers
- ❑ ledgers and other business records
- ❑ information on adoptions and evacuees

Skim quickly through this material, reminding yourself of the dramatic stories there that could be turned into a book.

What challenges do you think you might face? For example, does the mass of material seem so overwhelming that you fear getting bogged down in detail? Or are there unexplained mysteries and gaps? Don't get discouraged as all writers face some problems like this and there are established techniques for dealing with them. By working through *Family Fables* and undertaking the exercises suggested, you will continue to feel in control and will see your book through to the finish.

Drafting out your first plans

Sifting through your files will have left you buzzing with ideas and eager to begin, so it's time to draw up the first plans for your book. You'll need two sheets of paper and a pencil.

List of Events: Take a sheet of A4 lined paper and write down the margin the numbers 1 to 20. These represent the different chapters of your book, though of course you might eventually decide on more or fewer chapters. If you have a highly visual imagination, it might help to envisage the different stages of your book as scenes in a film. Against figure 1, write a sentence describing a suitable opening scene for your book. Against the figure 20, write a sentence describing the scene that will end your book. Now gradually fill in numbers 2 to 19 with episodes that get your family members from 1 to 20. The List of Events page is a first step towards ordering your material sequentially – what comes first, what comes next, and so on. As you progress through *Family Fables*, your List of Events will be modified and improved until it can act as the definitive Storyline for your book.

The Spidergram: Take another sheet of A4 paper and turn it lengthways, i.e. with the longest side of the paper at the bottom – 'landscape' rather than the usual 'portrait' orientation. Draw a circle in the centre of the page and write in it either the surname of the family line you are tracing or, if you are following the fate of just one family member, the principal character's name. Fill up the rest of the space on the page with key words for the topics and themes involved in your family history – e.g. farming, armed services, illness and death, position of women, inheritance, war, emigration, etc. Draw circles round these words and join the circles to each other (where appropriate) with straight lines to indicate the inter-relations of different themes. The themes can be connected to the central name with lines radiating out of the circle like spider's legs. The Spidergram page is a way of representing spatially the themes and topics you want to cover in your book.

These two sheets should only take twenty minutes each to write. You will modify and embellish these plans over and over again as you work your way through *Family Fables,* as you study your research in more detail, and as you experience 'Eureka!' moments when a bright idea occurs to you for organising the story a better way. The incidents on your List of Events can be viewed as the bare bones of your story, while the themes sketched out on your Spidergram are the flesh. As we shall see, arbitrating between the claims of the 'flesh' and the 'bones', the pattern and the life, is one of the main challenges facing writers.

Many family historians will be equipped with computers and tailor-made family history programs. These are a godsend as you can sort data at the touch of a button or click of a mouse. If your own research is still at the loose-paper-and-documents phrase, you will need to start sorting it so as to keep different topics separate. Because your first plans are provisional, be careful not to do anything irrevocable to your research notes. Colour-coding your notes with a streak of highlighter pen is useful at a later stage of the process, but don't disfigure the notes in this way (highlighter pen being hard to remove) until you've finished reading this book and made your final plans.

I suggest writing a code phrase, e.g. 'Domestic Service', in pencil on the top right-hand corner and paper-clipping the relevant pages together. It is not necessary to buy a lot of files and office equipment. Recycled manila envelopes in large sizes can be used to separate the different topics. You can write the title of that section on the envelope with a thick felt-tip pen and keep all the envelopes in a free cardboard box from the supermarket.

Some items will fall into more than one category. Cross-reference these by filing them in the most relevant envelope and placing dummy sheets in the other envelopes referring you back to the main location. As your book proceeds, you will certainly find yourself rubbing out the pencil marks and refiling the papers in different envelopes. This does not mean you have been wasting time: all writing involves exploration and you sometimes have to retrace your steps. You are learning every step of the way, which is something to celebrate, not to get frustrated about.

Framework of your book

Plots and openings are discussed in more detail in chapter 6. At this stage, you need to look at the research material you have gathered and consider broad angles for approaching your subject. You know you have the plot clearly in your mind when you can summarise it in one sentence.

Later chapters of *Family Fables* discuss different ways of telling your story, but you can start thinking like a writer now by asking yourself questions such as: How many characters and settings can I afford to include, before the reader gets lost? Who is the central character my readers can identify with? Which parts of my research lend themselves most readily to dramatic scenes with lots of tension and dialogue? What episodes would be best for a striking opening and for a satisfying conclusion? Perhaps some of the material will prove too awkward to be included in the main story and would be best consigned to an Appendix in the 'end-matter' (final pages) of the book – more advice on this in chapter 9.

Chronological order? The pros and cons

There must be some logical connection between the events you choose to include in your book, but the obvious principle of selection and organisation – chronological order – is not always the best. You might for example focus on an individual and his/her thoughts, feelings and experiences, so that *person* is the unifying factor that holds it all together, irrespective of the date order in which the material is delivered to the reader. Or you might concentrate on a *theme*, such as work or marriage, and organise all your material round that subject, finding contrasts and parallel situations. Character is discussed in the next chapter; for more on themes, see chapter 7.

Within a chronological framework, you have three basic choices. (1) The most straightforward way to tell a story is to write one simple narrative in chronological order. (2) A more sophisticated narrative might tell two or more simultaneous stories running in parallel and told in chronological order, so the plot is augmented by several sub-plots. (3) You could even write a series of separate narratives in chronological sequence, taking up characters one by one from different generations of your family, passing on the story like a baton in a race.

Most family historians take a chronological approach, albeit pursuing their research in *reverse* chronological order, starting with the present time and moving back into history. We do, after all, live life

understand it backwards, with the benefit
and perspective.

some thought to the chronological point from
ou start your family's story, as this can transform
the mood of the book, rather as a landscape appears
entirely different from the vantage point of one hill rather
than another.

So much for chronological order. Much modern
writing, however, both fiction and non-fiction, exhibits
disrupted chronology: events are related out of
chronological sequence with flashbacks to the past
and jumps ahead to the future. Literary fashion
aside, this technique has many benefits:

❏ You are free to place in meaningful juxtaposition
   events which took place at widely different times
   – even during different historical periods – and
   this can be useful if you are following a thematic
   thread through the book.
❏ Stories told out of chronological order demand
   more participation on the part of your readers.
   Transforming your readers into 'co-authors' in
   this way leads to deeper involvement and
   identification on their part.
❏ By withholding a key event, you can create a
   mystery which keeps readers turning the page
   until they solve it. You could, for example,
   describe an *effect* while withholding details of
   the *cause* of the effect. It is not only three-year-
   olds who endlessly want to know 'Why?'
❏ By interrupting the plot with sub-plots or
   flashbacks, you heighten the suspense as your
   readers progress through the book. Sub-plots

often involve characters who don't fully understand events in the main plot; interposing their (limited) viewpoint slows down the action and delays the resolution of any conflict in the primary action.

❑ You might even tell part of the story out of chronological order as a way of helping the reader understand the plot, revealing the facts about X only when readers *need* to know them and not before.

If you decide on a non-chronological telling of the story, you do not have to *write* it out of chronological sequence. It is often easier to write the first draft in linear fashion, then shuffle the chapters before embarking on the second and subsequent drafts.

Usually an event that happened once is narrated once, but you might decide to relate that incident several times, from the points of view of different characters. Conversely, an event that happens repeatedly (e.g. your great-great-grandfather going to work down the mine) can be narrated several times or only once, in summary. These decisions will affect the focus, mood and pace of the story, all of which are discussed in the chapters that follow.

Now that you have finished reading this chapter, you will probably want to go back to your first plans (the List of Events and the Spidergram) and modify them. The List of Events should be looking more and more like a Storyline with the incidents ordered according to where they will appear in your final draft. You have already started revising your own work – one of the most valuable skills a writer can learn. There will be more adjustments to make when we have looked at Character in the next chapter and Time in chapter 5.

Chapter 4: Choosing Characters

Character is the key to a biography. It is endlessly enjoyable to try and imagine what other people's lives might be like. Yet again, as a family historian-cum-writer you are in a privileged position. To a large extent your characters come to you ready-made: unlike a novelist you do not have to invent them from scratch. But the pen-portraits attached to your family tree still need to be fleshed out and have life breathed into them.

Think about how would you *feel* if you were in your ancestors' shoes – or clogs or fisherman's boots. How would you interpret what's happening to you? Visualise your characters, using photographs as a stimulus if possible, and give them thoughts to think and words to say. Try to get under their skin. A useful first step for all writers is to take a professional interest in the people around you – listen to them talking in supermarkets, in queues at the bank, waiting for a train. Keeping a writer's journal (discussed in chapter 11) is invaluable as you will learn about people by examining your own reaction to life. And as Socrates remarked, the unexamined life is not worth living.

Your characters must change in response to the ups and downs of the plot. When a character enters or leaves a scene, you should ask yourself, 'Where has this character come from? Where is he or she going? What do they want?' You also need to know exactly *who* knows *what,* at particular points in the story.

Based on the planning you did in chapter 3, you should be ready now to draw up a list of characters who will appear in your book – rather like the *dramatis personae* page at the front of a play. Many family historians have a database on their computer for collecting and handling information about known ancestors. If you prefer to work on paper, buy a pack of large index cards and write a character's name, in biro, across the top right-hand corner.   Draw a line vertically down the middle of the card and head the first half 'characteristics' and the second half 'actions'. Using a pencil, sketch out each character's personality in a few words or phrases in the left half and an outline of the scenes in which they appear on the right half. These cards (or your computer database) will provide an invaluable *aide-memoire* as you proceed through the book and you should keep adding to them.

Marginal characters such as neighbours, servants or employees can enrich your book as they place your family in context and introduce a new perspective. Who, after all, is not interested in what the butler saw? If a famous person came from the same village as your ancestor you could explore his or her career. Or choose someone else born the same year who had very different life experiences. As well as helping fill in the background, the experience of peripheral figures can tactfully fill in any gaps in your research.

Try to be imaginative in the way you introduce your characters. The protagonist does not have to appear in person on page one of the first chapter. You also need to decide to what extent your main characters will be revealed through their own words and to what extent through being described, either by other characters in the book or by you as the author. The different options for presenting characters can be broadly summarised as follows:

How will I introduce this character?

- ❑ In person
- ❑ In other people's conversation
- ❑ In a letter written by themselves
- ❑ In a letter by someone else

Think back to a novel or biography you have enjoyed. It is likely that you learnt about the characters in four different ways. (1) What the characters did. (2) What the characters thought, felt and said. (3) The quality of the characters' relationships with other people. (4) What other people (or the author) said about those characters. There are numerous examples in literature of writers using all these techniques. Dickens demonstrates the greed of Mr Bumble the Beadle in *Oliver Twist* by interspersing Bumble's words with actions:

'You are humane woman, Mrs Mann.' (Here she set down the glass.) 'I shall take an early opportunity of mentioning it to the board, Mrs Mann.' (He stirred the gin-and-water.) 'I – I drink your health with cheerfulness, Mrs Mann'; and he swallowed half of it.

Writers can also reveal a character's inner thoughts as a means of characterisation. In the following passage from *Sons and Lovers*, D H Lawrence shows us Mrs Morel's despair as she expects a third child she does not want:

But for herself, nothing but this dreary endurance – till the children grew up. And the children! She could not afford to have this third. She did not want it. The father was serving beer in a public-house, swilling himself drunk. She despised him, and was tied to him. This coming child was too much for her. If it were not for William and Annie, she was sick of it, the struggle with poverty and ugliness and meanness.

An author sometimes wishes to convey information about a character in a tactful, implicit manner, and recording the behaviour and conversation of other characters is ideal for this. Nancy, in *Oliver Twist,* is a prostitute. We learn this not through any actions or words of her own but from the ostentatious disgust directed at her by respectable domestic servants:

This allusion to Nancy's doubtful character raised a vast quantity of chaste wrath in the bosoms of four housemaids, who remarked with great fervour, that the creature was a disgrace to her sex; and strongly advocated her being thrown, ruthlessly, into the kennel …. Nancy remained, pale and almost breathless, listening with quivering lip to the very audible expressions of scorn, of which the chaste housemaids were very prolific …

Dickens is also the master of using small habits, verbal tics and clothing to characterise individuals economically. In the same novel, the Artful Dodger is always seen dressed grotesquely in adult clothing which is far too big for him. At a stroke, the artful Dickens has shown the reader that the boy has been thrown into adult vice before his time. Another of the criminals, Bill Sikes, is neatly identified by always being accompanied by his dog: '"What the devil's this?" said a man, bursting out of a beer-shop with a white dog at his heels.'

A superb passage in Mrs Gaskell's *North and South* explores a character's feelings, thoughts and actions to show his sense of hurt when a woman rejects his marriage proposal. Thornton is disorientated and Mrs Gaskell demonstrates the depth of his feeling by describing (without authorial comment) his irrational actions. The use of repetition in the passage expresses Thornton's numbness:

He could not bear the noise, the garish light, the continued rumble and movement of the street. He called himself a fool for suffering so; and yet he could not, at the moment, recollect the cause of his suffering, and whether it was adequate to the consequences it had produced. It would have been a relief to him, if he could have sat down and cried on a door-step by a little child, who was raging and storming, through his passionate tears, at some injury he had received…. There was an omnibus passing – going into the country; the conductor thought he was wishing for a place, and stopped near the pavement. It was too much trouble to apologise and explain; so he mounted upon it, and was borne away – past long rows of houses – then past detached villas with trim gardens, till they came to the real country hedge-rows, and, by-and-by, to a small country town. Then everybody got down; and so did Mr Thornton, and because they walked away he did so too.

This technique can be taken a step further and a character's feelings shown through 'stream of consciousness' writing. When Oliver Twist is shot and wounded during a bungled burglary and carried away from the scene of the crime, Dickens represents his

40

confused bodily sensations and numbed thoughts disconnectedly, using long sentences with lots of 'ands'. Mentioning 'uneven ground' is the masterstroke:

Then came the loud ringing of a bell, mingled with the noise of fire-arms, and the shouts of men, and the sensation of being carried over uneven ground at a rapid pace. And then, the noises grew confused in the distance; and a cold deadly feeling crept over the boy's heart; and he saw or heard no more.

As a rough rule of thumb, the more you use the 'inner thoughts' technique for characterisation, the more your readers will empathise with that character and want them to succeed. It is quite possible for readers to identify even with a bad person if you give enough insight into that person's inner life. By contrast, conveying character mainly through a person's actions, or the words of others, has a distancing effect: readers will respond to that character more objectively and less emotionally.

Whose Point of View?

The same story can be told in many different ways— this is a difference between the events of your story and the manner in which you choose to tell it. A very important choice concerns the point of view from which to tell your family's story. Don't begrudge the time spent deciding this. The relationship between the teller and the tale is fundamental, affecting the plot and tone of your book. If you get it wrong at the start, you will find yourself doing lots of rewriting which could have been avoided. Here are your choices:

(1) FIRST PERSON ACCOUNT, MAIN PROTAGONIST: If you sympathise with a central character in each generation, you could choose to write the story from his/her point of view, using the pronoun 'I'. This is called *first person* narration. It gives a vivid and intimate presentation of that person's life and the reader is likely to identify with him/her because of the insight into their emotions. However, you will be limited to describing events which that person might plausibly have experienced. Restricting the point of view to a single character in this way reduces the breadth of vision in a long book as the narrator – the 'I' – is unlikely to be physically present in all the important scenes. (You can get over this problem by having him or her receive letters or verbal accounts about incidents they did not witness, but this reduces the immediacy as information received in such a way is inevitably second-hand.) If such technical difficulties can be overcome, a first person account *in the present tense* is extremely powerful, as the international success of *Angela's Ashes* proves.

(2) FIRST PERSON ACCOUNT, BYSTANDER: An alternative is to choose a marginal character and tell the story from their point of view. For example, the story of the Towser family could be told through the eyes and ears of a comparatively powerless or peripheral member of that clan – a child, a poor relation, elderly servant, etc. Because the 'I' in this case is at one remove from the main action, this technique introduces an element of detachment.

The author can also ensure that a servant (say) is unobtrusively present during all the major scenes.

(3) THIRD PERSON ACCOUNT: It is more common to write a biography or family history in the third person, referring to the characters as 'he', 'she' and 'they'. This gives you, the writer, more control. You can still focus on one principal character and give their perspective on events, but that character won't be addressing the reader directly.

(4) INTRUSIVE AUTHOR TECHNIQUE: The method favoured by the great Victorian novelists was to give a panoramic view of a society or clan, with an omniscient author as it were hovering over the scene and able to switch at will from one perspective to another. The difference between a simple third person narrative (3) and the 'intrusive author' technique is that practitioners of this narrative form – George Eliot and Anthony Trollope, for example – periodically address the reader directly, in their own person as author, to comment on the characters and the action. Though for a long time considered old-fashioned, this technique began to come back into favour with novelists in the 1980s. It is a good approach for family historians faced with complicated material that is hard to organise and control. Some readers do not want to become co-authors but prefer the feeling of being 'in safe hands'.

To make sure you understand the difference between the four options above, think of three novels or biographies you have read and identify which technique the authors chose. The most popular choices are third person or intrusive author, but autobiographies are usually (not always!) written in the first person, and novelists have used bystander narratives (2) to subtle effect. For example, in *Wuthering Heights,* Emily Brontë uses a series of narrators who are characters in the book but not central to the action they describe.

At quite a deep level, *who* tells a story determines exactly *what* gets told: the values of your chosen narrator will influence their attitude to the subject matter and the words they use to describe it. The phrase 'point of view' implies value judgements as well as visual vantage point.

Accomplished authors can mix different points of view in the same novel, even in the same scene. The sheer energy and inventive genius of a Dickens, for example, are such that the reader usually does not notice the transitions. Less ambitious writers will find it easier to choose one narrative style at the planning stage and stick to it. If you are sure you want to present your family's story from more than one viewpoint, keep the chronology simple to compensate.

You should now be in a position to reconsider your original one-page plans, the List of Events and the Spidergram. What effect would different points of view have on your chosen events (in the List of Events) and themes (in the Spidergram)? For example, if a major event in your family was the First World War, and a major theme the pointless carnage of that conflict, it is unlikely you would choose to tell the story from the perspective of a domestic servant – a bystander character. That's not to say it couldn't be done, but it would make considerable demands on both writer and reader. Most writers, faced with this choice, would choose the third person approach.

Chapter 5: Time and Place

ABOUT TIME

As we saw in chapter 3, it is quite routine for modern-day biographers to write their subject's story in a way that deviates from chronology. When J R Ackerley wrote *My Father and Myself* (published 1968), this was by no means the case and he felt the need to explain and justify his practice in a Foreword to the book:

The apparently haphazard chronology of this memoir may need excuse. The excuse, I fear, is Art. It contains a number of surprises, perhaps I may call them shocks, which, as history, came to me rather bunched up towards the end of the story. Artistically shocks should never be bunched, they need spacing for maximum individual effect. To afford them this I could not tell my story straightforwardly and have therefore disregarded chronology and adopted the method of ploughing to and fro over my father's life and my own, turning up a little more sub-soil each time as the plough turned.

That Ackerley's apologia now seems unnecessary, even laboured, is a tribute to his own success in pioneering a new way of writing biography. The slightly puzzled tone shows that he was not altogether clear about what he was doing, or whether it was wise. Sometimes writers have to follow their own instincts and see where this leads them.

Even if you choose a basic year-by-year account, you will almost certainly need to allow some interruptions to the chronological sequence. For example, minor character X might appear briefly at one stage of your biographee's life but not have any significant effect on the plot until decades later. In this case it would be best to keep all your references to X in one part of the book because mentioning him fleetingly, in date order, will give your book a fragmentary and inconsequential feel. Again, certain themes such as parenting might be best handled in one section rather than continually interrupting the plot to report in parenthesis that a third child was born that year.

There is never a definitive right answer to the question, When is theme predominant and when should I concentrate on the sequence of events in time? Every case demands its own individual solution.

Your Timeline

Once again, it's time to take out your original plans, the List of Events/Storyline and the Spidergram. What period of time is needed to cover all the *events* on the List and to fully convey the *themes* on the Spidergram? Are you writing a saga covering several generations or a 'micro-biography', treating a short but dramatic period in the life of one of your forebears?

The third and final planning document you need is a Timeline. Take another sheet of A4 paper and place it on your desk with the longest side along the bottom. Draw a line along the bottom in black, an inch from the edge of the page, and write on the left-hand side of the line the date you expect to start your family's story. If you intend to start by focussing on one character, this may well be very precise, perhaps their date of birth – 23rd April 1854. Alternatively, you might choose (say) the decade in which the family firm was founded, or the family farm was sold, 1840s perhaps. On the far right of the line, write the date which will close your family history, e.g. the end of the Second World War, 1945.

Now divide up the line into sections representing periods of time between the 1840s and 1945. In this example, your timeline is about a century and you could divide it into twenty mini-eras of five years each. Now take a blue pen and, at appropriate intervals along the line, briefly record the main events in your family's history.

Finally, along the top of the sheet of paper, write in red pen the national and international events that formed the backdrop to your saga, placing these so they correspond to the dates written on the bottom of the sheet. For example the Reform Act of 1832 changed Parliament and hence British society, while the Married Women's Property Acts (1870 and 1882) improved the lives of many women. An event such as the Great Exhibition (1851) or the Boer Wars (1881, 1899) may also have been significant in the lives of your ancestors. By keeping a note of family events and national events on one document, you have an at-a-glance snapshot of the period your book covers.

Keep your Timeline in a plastic pocket with your List of Events/Storyline and Spidergram as you will be adding to it in chapter 6.

Flashbacks and Previews

Rather than summarising past events narratively, you can present them to the reader in the form of dramatic flashbacks. Visualise flashback scenes in as much detail as you can, including descriptions of the setting, the time of day and the season, what the characters are wearing, what they say, and so on. If you find you have a flair for flashbacks, you could write a series of them running throughout the whole narrative. This is more likely to engage the readers' interest than a chronological plod through characters' lives with large amounts of information divulged in one go.

Flashbacks deepen our understanding of characters' true personalities and they are often introduced at turning-points in the characters' fortunes. *Middlemarch* by George Eliot features a sub-plot about a banker who is afraid the sordid origins of his wealth might become public. Eliot uses a flashback to reveal to the reader hitherto unknown facts about his life:

Night and day, without interruption save of brief sleep which only wove retrospect and fear into a fantastic present, he felt the scenes of his earlier life coming between him and everything else, as obstinately as when we look through the window from a lighted room, the objects we turn our backs on are still before us, instead of the grass and the trees.... Once more he saw himself the young banker's clerk.... That was the happiest time of his life: that was the spot he would have chosen now to awake in and find the rest a dream. [and so on, for several pages]

Before describing a character's death, an author can remind readers of the plot to date and look back over the dying one's life in flashback. Alternatively, you could change the point of view at this stage and allow the reader to see the character through the eyes of someone who will survive them.

As well as flashbacks, writers occasionally add variety by jumping ahead in the story to provide omens and hints of events to come. Previews of events that have not yet taken place are effective for increasing the tension and making readers aware of the passage of time, its inevitability and inherent sadness. In *Oliver Twist*, Nancy foretells her death at the hands of Bill Sikes and shows she is powerless to escape: 'Whether it is God's wrath for the wrong I have done, I do not know; but I am drawn back to him through every suffering and ill usage; and I should be, I believe, if I knew that I was to die by his hand at last.'

Transitions - the passage of time

A common weakness in novice writing is giving all facts, and all periods of time, the same weight and space. It is no more necessary to describe every year in detail than it is to describe every journey in exhaustive detail. In *Precious Bane*, novelist Mary Webb moves from close-up to long-shot when a new chapter opens in summary style, accounting for six months in a few lines. Reference to the cycle of the seasons and growth of crops unobtrusively indicates the passing of time:

From the time when Jancis when to Callard's Dingle, through the spring and summer, there is nothing written in my book saving of my own special concerns, such as the progress I made in reading hard books and the thoughts that came to me in the attic.... Gideon went to Callard's Dingle every Sunday, and worked like three men in between. I ploughed furrow for furrow ahead of him, and dug spade for spade. Our farm was rich with corn.

Several years pass in the 'gaps' between different chapters of Dickens' *Great Expectations.* Sometimes the passage of time is indicated with a plain statement to prepare the way for a major scene or twist in the plot. Here are some examples:

I was in the fourth year of my apprenticeship to Joe, and it was a Saturday night. (Start of chapter 18)

As I am now generalising a period of my life with the object of clearing my way before me, I can scarcely do so better than by at once completing the description of our usual manners and customs at Barnard's Inn. (Chapter 34)

I was three-and-twenty years of age. Not another word had I heard to enlighten me on the subject of my expectations, and my twenty-third birthday was a week gone. We had left Barnard's Inn more than a year and lived in the Temple. (Start of chapter 39)

At other times, Dickens punctuates his story with a brief reflective or philosophical passage at the start of a new chapter. These moments of calm enable the reader to view the action from a wider, and wiser, perspective:

It is a most miserable thing to feel ashamed of home. There may be black ingratitude in the thing, and the punishment may be retributive, and well deserved; but, that it is a miserable thing, I can testify. (Start of chapter 14)

I now fell into a regular routine of apprenticeship-life, which was varied, beyond the limits of the village and the marshes, by no more remarkable circumstance than the arrival of my birthday and my paying another visit to Miss Havisham. (Start of chapter 17)

Epilogues

Although your Timeline might end in (say) 1945, readers may well be interested in hearing of the future destiny of your family, and this additional material can be placed in an Epilogue, which usually stands alone and is not given a chapter number. This is a handy way of tidying up loose details without spoiling a thematic pattern or ending the main part of the book on an anticlimax.

Although time can be viewed as the source of pain, since it inevitably involves loss, it is also a great healer. You can bring your book to an emotionally satisfying conclusion by relating events long after the trauma you have recounted, giving a sense of the 'calm after the storm'. The dead have a prolonged influence on the living, and a meditation on this theme can be a consoling and fitting end to a book.

PLACE

Your choice of setting – where, geographically, to concentrate your family's story – will influence other elements of your book. Setting affects the mood and atmosphere of a book, and certain choices of setting could exclude types of characters, for example those belonging to certain social classes, or one or other of the sexes.

You can add an extra layer of meaning by discussing the history of a place and the primitive people who occupied the land. In *The Mayor of Casterbridge,* Thomas Hardy sets significant scenes on the Roman foundations of the town, deepening our sense of the timelessness and inevitability of the mayor's fate.

Humour can be introduced by exploring different characters' response to the same place, as Smollett does in *Humphry Clinker*, contrasting a young girl's passion for fashionable Bath with the sour animadversions of a middle-aged man who hates all the parties.

Important though setting is, descriptions of nature can be overdone and you will bore the reader if you continue in this vein for more than a couple of paragraphs at a time. Instead of dealing with setting, action and dialogue in separate blocks, vary and lighten your writing by weaving the different elements together in the same passage. You can add further interest by referring to how the scene appeals to the different senses of the characters. Perhaps the sun *feels* hot on Lydia's skin and she can *smell* crushed grass and *hear* birds singing as she *tastes* the wild berries and *watches* the patterns of light and shade made by leaves in the wind. If it is windy, her hair may be blown across her face and she will need to brush it back, perhaps with a hand stained with the juice of berries. Entering into Lydia's experience in this way will help your readers imagine what it must feel like to be Lydia in that setting. It is a vastly more intimate technique than describing what she can see in the form of a static list.

To fully appreciate the places that played a significant part in your family's history, there is no substitute for a personal visit. Going to their home town or village and wandering round (say) the parish church can help you to capture the atmosphere of their daily lives. Some excellent biographies have been written by a researcher who has literally walked in the footsteps of the subject. For his long study of Garibaldi, historian G M Trevelyan walked over every inch of Italian soil that Garibaldi had covered with his army. History is brought to life as Trevelyan describes the heat, rough hillsides, scent of herbs, and so on that Garibaldi himself would have experienced on his campaigns.

On a visit to your family's home territory, listen out for any local folklore and check back issues of local newspapers for anything (not only obituaries) that might shed light on contemporary behaviour and attitudes during your ancestors' era. If possible, visit a place at the same time of year and the same time of day that your ancestor was there. If he or she wrote anything about the place, in a letter or diary, copy out these words on the left-hand page of an exercise book and write your own impressions on the facing right-hand page.

Try to make the visit in a calm and reflective state of mind and pay attention to *all* your sense impressions: what does the place smell like? what can you hear? is it unbearably hot or uncomfortably cold? If the significant place is a building and your ancestor was a domestic servant, try getting on your knees and pondering what she would see from that perspective, while scrubbing the floor. What would she do with her long skirts to stop them trailing over bits of the floor that were wet and soapy? Which parts of her body ached most?

Transitions - movement through space

If a journey forms part of your story, think very carefully about how much of that journey needs to be recorded. Is anything important said or done on the journey? Perhaps the boredom and confinement of a coach or railway carriage leads to confession. The characters might feel liberated from their normal setting and able to discuss private matters in an unreserved fashion. Alternatively, you might want an opportunity to describing local scenery viewed through the carriage window.

On the other hand, if there happens to be no reason for turning the journey into a scene in your book, you can make the transition from one location to another as perfunctory as you wish. Here is Dickens moving Nancy rapidly from a scene in Fagin's kitchen (where she is under discussion) to a police station:

While these, and many other encomiums, were being passed on the accomplished Nancy, that young lady made the best of her way to the police-office; whither, notwithstanding a little natural timidity consequent upon walking through the streets alone and unprotected, she arrived in perfect safety shortly afterwards.

Since there is no plot-related or character-related reason for the writer to dwell on Nancy's journey through the streets, and the setting has already been described, Dickens achieves the scene-change with minimum fuss.

As author, you have the power to compress or expand time and space according to the overall needs of the plot. The plot is what we shall examine next.

Chapter 6: Plot, Conflict and Tension

Plots are what keep readers interested. You can have a poem without a plot but an extended piece of creative prose must have action and development. As researcher, you collected and recorded the scattered facts about your family's progress; with your writer's hat on, it is now your task to orchestrate those events into a story. Novelists complain of the difficulty of finding plots for their novels, but family historians usually find they have the opposite problem – there are so many extraordinary true stories in their boxes of research that they are spoilt for choice. Here are ten themes that feature in many family sagas, any one of which could form the genesis of a dramatic plot. Your own family story might include all of these, and you can probably think of twenty more.

❑ Portrait of a time and place, a lost world
❑ Clogs and shawls: the local community, chapel-going, trade unions, working men's clubs
❑ A gifted child is born: a new human being enters history
❑ The parents' lives: men's work, women's work
❑ The child's education
❑ Conflict: the main character's battle with society/other people/his own nature
❑ Emigration, war, the armed forces, domestic service
❑ First job: learning the ropes, the jargon of different trades
❑ Courtship and marriage customs
❑ Death and its aftermath; reading the will

Take out the Timeline which you wrote for Chapter 5 on Time and Place. Referring to your List of Events/ Storyline for guidance, pencil on to the Timeline the peaks and troughs of the drama in your plot, with 'mountains' for the scenes of climax and 'valleys' for the quieter passages. You need a vivid opening scene, several confrontations and a resolution at the end. You will probably find you wish to update and modify the Storyline at this point, taking into account the importance of drama at fairly regular intervals. The climactic scenes will be written in close-up, with lots of dialogue and description, while the reflective scenes can be quieter and might encompass months, even years, of time. These transitional passages are the perfect place for introducing your own narrative voice, outlook and philosophy.

The plot doesn't have to be original. In fact there is no such thing as a new plot. Every conceivable story-line has been done before, which probably tells us something about the human condition. A standard plot can be enlivened by interesting, strongly motivated characters or an unusual setting. All human beings want to read about other human beings overcoming hardship, enduring suffering, taking big risks. The 'triumphing over disadvantage' template, coupled with interesting characters and background, can hardly fail.

If you feel stuck in any part of the plot, try starting the story from a different point in time or from another character's viewpoint. You are still at the planning stage and nothing in your Storyline, Spidergram or Timeline is set in stone.

Seven Basic Plots?

Going back to Dr Samuel Johnson in the eighteenth century, literary theorists have conjectured that all of the stories in the world boil down to a handful of archetypes. There are many variants of this theory, but seven is a popular number:

1.   Unrecognised virtue is at last rewarded.
2.   A fatal flaw leads the hero to his doom.
3.   Fate of the hero when his good luck turns bad.
4.   A man and a woman meet and fall in love.
5.   The hero faces a series of obstacles and overcomes them all.
6.   An innocent person gets entangled with a villain and is hurt.
7.   The eternal triangle: two men and one woman or vice versa.

Although these plots can be traced back to the dawn of civilisation, they feature in literature published every week. You may well find yourself viewing your ancestors' histories through one of these 'lenses'.

Genres

A visit to your local bookshop will demonstrate that popular genres of writing include romance, horror, gothic horror, crime, detective stories, spy fiction, nostalgia/historical, regional sagas, sci-fi and fantasy. This 'category fiction' sells in its hundreds of thousands and non-fiction writers have much to learn from it. Your research could perhaps be written up as a regional saga, a rags to riches story or a romance.

A 'whodunit' treatment might suit your family story. Was Uncle Ezekiel really eaten by cannibals or could there be some other less exotic – or even more surprising – explanation for his disappearance? A family story that could be written up as a mystery in this way would allow you to conceal some of the facts from your readers for most of the book, increasing their curiosity so that they keep turning the pages, wanting to know more.

Using the Romance Genre

If your ancestors were from humble backgrounds, they could have married for love rather than for dynastic reasons, such as adding to the property and importance of the family. If a courtship and marriage is central to any part of your family's story, you could explore the conventions of writing romance. Where would your young people have met – chapel? the market? How mobile were they and how likely was it that they might meet a partner from a different village or region?

A romantic framework is perfect for writers who don't wish to have *too* many decisions to make. The conventions are well-established. The usual way to open a romantic story is at a turning-point in the life of the heroine. She will often be depicted discussing her future with a confidante – a friend or trusted servant, perhaps. The conflict and tension in a romantic story derives from some force that keeps the couple apart. It may be a longstanding family feud or something as apparently trivial as a misunderstanding at a party. Your plot then traces the gradual removal of the obstacle or false belief. In *Pride and Prejudice*, we see the collapse of Darcy's pride as he admits to himself he loves Elizabeth, and the melting away of Elizabeth's prejudice when she realises Darcy is a considerate man, not the arrogant monster she has taken him to be.

Sub-plots and multiple plots

Fiction is enriched by the addition of subsidiary story-lines, or sub-plots, which interact with the main action – sometimes mirroring it, sometimes providing a stark contrast. A sub-plot is ideal for reminding readers of minor characters. It can also help you control the pace: if you want to end a chapter as a cliff-hanger, it is pointless to resolve the tension in the next chapter, so turning to a sub-plot can keep your readers in suspense for a chapter or two.

A master of the multiple plot was Victorian author Anthony Trollope who wrote two series of linked novels where each book stands alone but features some of the same characters as the other novels in the series. Trollope's novel sequences about Victorian politics (the Palliser series) and life in a cathedral town (the Barsetshire series) form a comprehensive overview of middle-class Victorian life and hurry the reader from one plot-line to the next. As the examples below show, Trollope used the 'intrusive author' technique. The reader is left in no doubt about who is in charge of the many stories that make up his novels.

Not disappointed with his achievement Mr Slope went his way. He first posted the precious note which he had in his pocket, and then pursued other enterprises in which we must follow him in other chapters. (*Barchester Towers,* chapter 26)

We will now follow Mr Slope so as to complete the day with him, and then return to his letter and its momentous fate in the next chapter. (*Barchester Towers,* chapter 27)

In this way, Trollope keeps readers' interest by making them wait for the unfolding fate of Mr Slope and the other characters. A shorter way of handling multiple plots is to treat simultaneously (i.e. in the same time-frame) events occurring in different places, bringing these events together in a single paragraph:

The bishop of Barchester said grace over the well-spread board in the Ullathorne dining-room; and while he did so the last breath was flying from the dean of Barchester as he lay in his sick room in the deanery. When the bishop of Barchester raised his first glass of champagne to his lips, the deanship of Barchester was a good thing in the gift of the prime minister. Before the bishop of Barchester had left the table, the minister of the day was made aware of the fact at his country seat in Hampshire, and had already turned over in his mind the names of five very respectable aspirants for the preferment. (*Barchester Towers*, chapter 38)

Multiple plots are now routine in modern 'literary' novels (the kind that win prizes) and readers expect several stories running at once.

Showing and Telling

Creative writing students are always entreated to 'show, don't tell'. 'Showing' involves dramatic scenes with lots of action and speech; 'telling', a summary of the action. Compare the following:

TELLING: She was angry and frightened the child.
SHOWING: She slammed the door shut and approached the boy, yelling, 'I've told you before, I won't put up with this!' Moaning uncomprehendingly, he backed away from her and knocked over a chair.

In reality you need a variety of passages – some dramatic scenes and some reflective or philosophical sections. Summarising and philosophising can come as a welcome relief from action, too much of which can lend a jerky, melodramatic feeling to a story.

A literary example of this 'telling' is the opening passage of Oliver Goldsmith's classic novel *The Vicar of Wakefield* where the vicar looks back over his married life and summarises it in a paragraph:

I was ever of opinion, that the honest man who married and brought up a large family, did more service than he who continued single and only talked of population. From this motive, I had scarce taken orders a year, before I began to think seriously of matrimony, and chose my wife, as she did her wedding-gown, not for a fine glossy surface, but such qualities as would wear well. To do her justice, she was a good-natured, notable woman; and as for breeding, there were few country ladies who could show more. She could read any English book without much spelling; but for pickling, preserving, and cookery, none could excel her. She prided herself also upon being an excellent contriver in housekeeping; though I could never find that we grew richer with all her contrivances.

This sets the leisurely and good-humoured tone of the book but is hardly dramatic. Taken to its logical conclusion, a whole book in the manner of this introduction would become an essay, speech or sermon, not a story. Ernest Hemingway's short stories are at the opposite extreme – no past, no setting, no philosophical overview but simply direct action and dialogue presented with immediacy.

In short, too much action and the story will seem jerky, melodramatic, improbable; too little and your reader will be bored. Take the formulas recommended by creative writing textbooks (e.g. 70% showing to 30% telling) with a pinch of salt. You are the author and should not be dictated to about the ratio of action/ dialogue to summary in your book. Be guided by your own judgement.

Openings, middles, crises

It is vital to open your book in a way that makes the reader want to read on. One way to start your story is *in medias res*, which means 'in the middle of things'. Many novels start with an abnormal moment of high drama, then the next chapter fills in the background and portrays the normal state of affairs.

You might want to make a sweeping philosophical statement, then descend to the particular; or reverse the procedure, starting with a small incident then broadening out. Other striking ways to open your book include a question apparently addressed to the reader; a quirky line of dialogue that doesn't seem to make sense; or a shocking statement, such as this from *South Riding* by Winifred Holtby where she introduces new characters with the words:

When Tom Sawdon bought the Nag's Head on the road between Maythorpe and Cold Harbour, he did not know that it would kill his wife.

The centre of your book will probably consist of small briskly described scenes leading up to a crisis. The very early chapters have to contain a lot of explanatory material but once the setting and characters are established, your reader will want to be drawn towards an exciting action scene. The big scene does not need to be a matter of life and death. In closed and static communities, the loss of someone's reputation, a failed love affair or the start of a family feud can be as catastrophic as the loss of life.

Conflict and suspense

Conflict and suspense should be present to some degree in any story. It has been said that 'happiness writes white', meaning that it is hard to make a page-turner out of a state of contentment. A simple framework would be to identify in your central character an ambition and examine the barriers that stood in their way and had to be overcome. The ambition can be a moving-towards ambition (she longed to become a governess to a noble family) or a moving-away ambition (her urge to escape the poverty and ignorance of the mining village into which she was born). The central issue may be one of life and death or simply the 'spiritual death' of not fulfilling one's potential. Conflict comes in three varieties:

- ❑ A character pitted against nature or society at large
- ❑ A character pitted against other people, e.g. battles with authority figures
- ❑ A character struggling with his/her own nature, e.g. lack of confidence or education

If you look back at your research, you will often find family members facing such challenges as the unemployment or death of a bread-winner, business failure, family break-up through adultery or divorce, and so forth. How did your ancestors surmount the obstacles on their paths and reach their goals? How did they face up to their own weaknesses, the jealousy or malice of others, the conditions and prejudices of their times, to forge ahead achieve their dreams? What was the outcome?

Sigmund Freud once observed his tiny grandson repeatedly throwing a toy out of his pram and pulling it back on a string, chanting to himself '*Fort* ... *Da*' ('Gone away ... Here'). Stripped to the absolute basics, all narratives conform to the Fort-Da framework: a state of loss is followed by either restoration or a coming to terms with that loss. Many of your family's stories could be approached as examples of this most fundamental patterning. Loss and its consequences offer innumerable opportunities for narrative drive.

Revelations

The uncovering of a secret can have the same energising effect on the plot as action, and there is less risk of melodrama. A mere letter, possibly couched in polite terms, can detonate a bomb in someone's life. Perhaps a character discovers that he is illegitimate or that his inheritance comes not from respectable sponsors but from a criminal, as Dickens' protagonist Pip discovers in *Great Expectations.* Such new knowledge utterly transforms Pip's prospects and his life is never the same again. Losing one's illusions and learning the truth can feel like being hit by a train.

In George Eliot's novel *Middlemarch,* the young widow Dorothea walks unannounced into a married woman's drawing-room and discovers her own suitor, Will Ladislaw, in a compromising position with Mrs Rosamond Lydgate. The accidental conjunction of these three people in one room leads to no outbursts, but the moral effect on all three is shattering:

She found herself on the other side of the door without seeing anything remarkable, but immediately she heard a voice speaking in low tones which startled her ... and advancing unconsciously a step or two beyond the projecting slab of a bookcase, she saw, in the terrible illumination of a certainty which filled up all outlines, something which made her pause motionless, without self-possession enough to speak. Seated with his back towards her on a sofa which stood against the wall on a line with the door by which she had entered she saw Will Ladislaw: close by him and turned towards him with a flushed tearfulness which gave a new brilliancy to her face sat Rosamond, her bonnet hanging back, while Will leaning towards her clasped both her upraised hands in his and spoke with low-toned fervour.

George Eliot allows the reader to follow Dorothea out of the room on her quiet way home, and mutual recriminations between Rosamond and Will are delayed until the next chapter; but the plot has a new impetus and direction simply because of what Dorothea has silently observed.

Suspense and Tension

Tension arises from uncertainty – keeping some information, or the ultimate outcome, hidden from the reader. Your readers should be kept wanting to turn the page and should be surprised when they have done so. However, you as the writer must be sure at every point how much each character knows about the subject at issue. If you're not clear about this, your characters' motivation will be confused and you will not carry your readers with you.

In *Return of the Native,* novelist Thomas Hardy wants the reader to experience Eustacia's longing for Clem, who has returned to Wessex from Paris. The suspense is increased when she fails five times to see him walking on the heath and has to resort to going to his mother's house in disguise and peeping at him while she lies on the floor, acting a part in the Mummers' play. By the time this point is reached, the reader is as desperate to see Clem as Eustacia is!

Pace

Another novel by Thomas Hardy uses rapid fragmentary scenes to add pace and excitement. Chapter 52 of *Far From The Madding Crowd* is divided into seven very short scenes depicting different people getting ready for Boldwood's Christmas party, where Boldwood will shoot Troy dead. The short scenes occur in different settings and involve different characters:

1. Boldwood's house is prepared for the party.
2. Bathsheba gets dressed.
3. Boldwood gets dressed.
4. Troy talks to a crony in a tavern.
5. Bathsheba discusses her unwillingness to marry.
6. Boldwood tells Gabriel Oak that he wants to marry Bathsheba.
7. Troy dons a disguise to wear at the party.

The reader feels breathless and apprehensive after having been whirled rapidly from one busy scene to another in this short chapter. The stage is obviously set for a crisis.

By contrast, short episodes of minimal drama and *no* apparent importance can slow down the pace and delay the start of major plot event, setting up a sense of uneasy anticipation in the reader.

Using even greater subtlety, you could advance your plot by avoiding a major scene altogether, merely hinting at what has occurred. This can also imply, perhaps for humorous effect, that the scene is too violent to bear description. When the bishop of Barchester's redoubtable wife, Mrs Proudie, decides to give him a severe telling-off in *Barchester Towers,* author Anthony Trollope shrinks from describing the combat in the conjugal bedroom:

There are some things which no novelist, no historian, should attempt; some few scenes in life's drama which even no poet should dare to paint. Let that which passed between Dr Proudie and his wife on this night be understood to be among them. He came down the following morning a sad and thoughtful man.

And so the plot moves on.

Now it's time to take out the Spidergram once again and consider how to handle theme.

Chapter 7: Theme

Every book involves a balancing act between the particular and the general, content and shape, events and the pattern imposed on them. Plot and action give a book human interest value; general themes elevate its status from a disjointed set of notes to a coherent work of art. You will find yourself constantly negotiating between the foreground and the background and trying to give proper attention and weight to both the 'wood' and the 'trees'.

It is important to avoid treating theme as entirely separate from the plot or story, handling it in lumps like a school essay. This technique was used by the very earliest English novelists in the eighteenth century. Henry Fielding, for example, repeatedly interrupts the plot of *Tom Jones* to interject his own views. While this works for an author of Fielding's calibre, it inevitably reduces the reader's identification with characters. You risk destroying all illusion and diminishing the characters to the status of puppets dancing to the writer's tune.

Themes can be communicated through careful choice of figurative language from a particular sphere of activity, using the vocabulary of (say) agriculture, religion or finance. You can signal the theme of your book through your choice of title and chapter headings. Catchy titles can be found in books of proverbs or quotations, folk songs and pop songs, hymnbooks, poetry, or Bible passages. Obvious chapter headings such as dates or place names don't do much to draw the reader in, so try something more daring. You could perhaps organise material according to certain deadly sins and cardinal virtues apparent in your characters' lifestyles, or use their nicknames.

Themes and motifs (mini themes) might relate to concrete objects, such as the tools of a trade or an heirloom – a physical presence that appears repeatedly in the book, in different circumstances and periods of time. The heirloom might represent a lost fortune, the tools could stand for the dignity of manual work, or the skill of a craftsman. Other themes are less tangible and can be expressed in a single abstract noun such as 'success', 'ambition', 'justice', 'oppression' or 'loyalty'.

In her novel about industrial England in the Victorian period, *North and South,* Mrs Gaskell several times uses noise, or the absence of it, to create atmosphere. In the following passage sound adds to the sense of dread as workers carry the body of a colleague who has committed suicide in his despair:

Gathering, gathering along the narrow street, came a hollow, measured sound; now forcing itself on their attention. Many voices were hushed and low: many steps were heard, not moving onwards, at least not with any rapidity or steadiness of motion, but as if circling round one spot. Yes, there was one distinct, slow tramp of feet, which made itself a clear path through the air, and reached their ears; the measured, laboured walk of men carrying a heavy burden. They were all drawn towards the house-door by some irresistible impulse; impelled thither – not by a poor curiosity, but as if by some solemn blast.

The bustle of the industrial north is one of the themes of this novel; Mrs Gaskell's use of noise and silence as a thread running through the book is a subtle way of unifying the story.

More explicitly, in *Anna of the Five Towns*, novelist Arnold Bennett focuses on the connections between money and nonconformist Christianity in the Potteries region of mid-Victorian England. Not all the chapel-goers are sincere, and the hypocrisy of those who treat religion as a business is exposed. A related theme is the tyranny of the Victorian paterfamilias in the home: power has to some extent corrupted family life as well as religion. This exercise of power is thrown into relief by the 'meekness' (this word recurs) of more unfortunate characters. Early in the book we are told, 'Blessed are the meek, blessed are the failures, blessed are the stupid, for they, unknown to themselves, have a grace which is denied to the haughty, the successful, and the wise.' The theme appears in the very last sentence of the novel, where Bennett reveals that a meek character has committed suicide and the world is 'the poorer by a simple and meek soul stung to revolt only in its last hour'.

Thomas Hardy's *Mayor of Casterbridge* is steeped in symbols and repeatedly uses imagery relating to the colour gold. The mayor makes his fortune selling golden corn, is invested with the mayor's gold chain of office, and his final defeat is signalled symbolically by the death of a goldfinch that he tries, and fails, to give to his estranged daughter as a wedding present.

Despite the popular conception of *Wuthering Heights,* few of the climactic scenes in that novel take place in the open air. The book's pervasive sense of rugged northern countryside is achieved through verbal imagery on the themes of wild animals and dramatic weather. Emily Brontë's figurative references to nature convince the reader that the countryside is omnipresent in the plot, which is not the case.

Family historians with a great span of history to encompass may be impatient with this emphasis on verbal embellishment. It is certainly true that readers of prose, whether fiction or non-fiction, are interested first and foremost in the events depicted, rather than on the manner in which those events are communicated. Unlike poetry, prose does give at least the impression of being a transparent medium. Nevertheless, a well-crafted piece of prose that is rhythmic and harmonious in some sections, abrupt and explosive in others, and where the style mirrors the content, is more effective in moving and engaging the reader than prose flatly recording a series of events. The language of your book needs to match both its content and the proposed readership.

We shall be looking at a range of literary techniques in the next chapter and there are exercises in chapter 11 to help you develop your creative writing skills. However, if you are embarrassed by 'purple passages' and want your book to tell a story and nothing else, take heart. Some of the greatest English writers, from Daniel Defoe to George Orwell, cultivated a style that was principally informative rather than poetic.

Chapter 8: The writer's toolkit – how to do things with words

Tone and level

The planning stage involves not only outlining the content of your book but also choosing a suitable style for your target readership. Having a notional 'perfect reader' in mind will help you to pitch your book at the right level of difficulty. Some jargon or dialect terms need explanation but other expressions will be easily understood by any literate adult and you don't want to patronise your reader by explaining them. Like so much of the craft of writing, these choices are a matter of balance and good judgement.

Information on the habits and trades of days gone by is very valuable and will enhance your book provided it can be presented dramatically, not in the form of a lecture. The data could be conveyed by introducing a newcomer who needs to be shown the ropes. An experienced worker, long-term resident of the village, etc., can induct the novice into 'the way we do things round here' in a scene including action and dialogue. Most of us would rather be told a story than be lectured at.

Textbooks sometimes refer to a writer's 'tone'. This is similar to someone's tone of voice when they speak to you. It conveys the writer's (or speaker's) attitude both to you, the listener, and to their subject matter. Even if you try to write very objectively and keep yourself out of the story, it is practically impossible for a writer to conceal his or her own attitudes and values. All writing involves selection, and what you include and leave out is highly revealing. Sensitive readers can always detect the author's tone in a piece of extended writing, so try to ensure your 'tone of voice' in addressing the reader and the subject matter is appropriate to what you are trying to do in the book. If your book is intended to be a heart-warming story of ordinary folk triumphing over their difficulties, the tone should be uplifting and positive, not satirical.

Ways of Recording Speech

Having your characters talk is one of the best ways of bringing your story to life. The most dynamic way of representing characters' conversations is direct speech, but there are other choices.

1. DIRECT SPEECH consists of actual quoted words within speech marks. E.g: 'May I have some more coal, Mr Scrooge?' asked Cratchit.

2. REPORTED SPEECH summarises a character's speech without using their actual words. E.g: Cratchit asked Scrooge politely for some coal.

3. FREE INDIRECT SPEECH uses the actual words selected by the character but no quotation marks are needed and the reader understands that the words may remain unspoken, being part of the character's 'interior monologue' or silent thoughts. E.g: Hopeless asking Scrooge for more coal! Cratchit stirred his fire gingerly.

4. 'SUBMERGED' or 'COLOURED' discourse: This involves writing a piece of *third-person* narrative but using the habitual words, phrases and verbal tics of the *character* whose speech is indicated. This gives you, the author, full control over the narrative while allowing your reader access to the consciousness of one of the characters. It therefore has some of the benefits of a first person narrative – intimacy and immediacy – but doesn't involve sacrificing authorial control.

Dickens often uses this technique of 'verbal signature' when he wants to distance us from a character or institution he dislikes. His account of the Poor Law guardians in *Oliver Twist* uses submerged discourse for ironic effect:

So, they established the rule, that all poor people should have the alternative (for they would compel nobody, not they), of being starved by a gradual process in the house, or by a quick one out of it.

In the same novel, Dickens makes humorous use of reported speech (type 2 above), demonstrating how Fagin's rather formal verbal style disguises threats as small talk:

Mr Fagin concluded by drawing a rather disagreeable picture of the discomforts of hanging; and, with great friendliness and politeness of manner, expressed his anxious hopes that he might never be obliged to submit Oliver Twist to that unpleasant operation.

By choosing one of these options for speech, you can control how close your readers get to the characters. Direct speech, as the phrase suggests, is a direct representation of the character's own words whereas reported speech, coloured speech or free indirect speech all give the author more control over 'pattern' in the overall work.

Letters are a useful way of conveying someone's character as they reveal a person's idiosyncratic speech habits. Letters from one character to another are an unobtrusive way of recapping the plot, so the reader doesn't get lost, and can link together sub-plots taking place in different parts of the country.

In addition to choosing how to represent characters' speech (direct speech, reported speech, etc.) you need to write speech in such a way that it sounds spontaneous but is interesting in its own right and moves the story along. In real life, unplanned speech is often rambling, ungrammatical and allusive so that an authentic transcript of a spontaneous conversation would be confusing and boring to read. The best way to pick up the knack of writing dialogue is to study the techniques used by fiction writers. Go back to a favourite novel – whether it's a great Victorian classic or a modern thriller doesn't matter – and examine how the author uses speech to convey character and plot.

It is quite acceptable to repeat 'he said' and 'she said' when recording your characters' speech. These phrases are so colourless that your readers don't notice them and drawing attention to them by writing 'she snarled', 'he divulged', 'she tittered' is pointless and distracting. However, it is sometimes effective to interrupt a comment *mid-sentence* with 'he said' at a carefully chosen point. Where you place the pause can make a difference to the overall tone of the passage.

The chain of 'he saids' and 'she saids' should not be too long anyway, as you will of course be interspersing your dialogue with movements. A long conversation could be broken up with the statement, 'Jeremiah threw off his coat' followed by a line of dialogue. It will be obvious from the position of the line of dialogue, immediately after Jeremiah's action, that it is Jeremiah who is speaking, so this line does not need the 'he said' tag at all.

Conversations longer than a page can be difficult for the reader to follow without counting back to see who is speaking. Get over this problem by having the speaker indicate, at intervals, the name or status of the person they are addressing: 'Begging your pardon, sir, but I don't think it will be possible.' 'Look here, Lois, I think we'd better get one thing straight.'

If your characterisation is thorough and convincing, the reader should be able to work out who is speaking from the dialogue alone, as we all have our favourite vocabulary and verbal style. Think of the various utterances of Alfred Jingle in Dickens' *Pickwick Papers* or Joe Gargery in *Great Expectations*. They could be spoken by no-one else.

Dialect and 'period' speech

Ambitious writers may wish to study the speech habits peculiar to the geographical region(s) their family inhabited or the historical period in which the plot is based, to give the dialogue extra authenticity. This is not to be undertaken lightly. A tiny mistake in dialect, or an anachronistic use of a slang expression, can destroy all credibility and your readers will stop believing in the plot. Too much 'fie, fie!' and 'methinks' can also sound comical.

Your book might include a vast cast of characters and it would certainly be convenient to use language styles as an indicator of class and status. Educated characters could be made to speak the Queen's English while the working classes used more homely words. However, although your family might have used dialect words and expressions at home amongst friends and neighbours, they were probably 'bilingual' and capable of speaking standard English when talking to authority figures such as the boss, the vicar and the schoolmistress. Any appearances in court would bring out your ancestors' 'Sunday speech', just as there were special Sunday clothes that would never be worn on a working day. If you should be lucky enough to have a verbatim example of an ancestor's speech patterns, such as a transcript of court proceedings, this will of course be an invaluable guide to writing dialogue in your book. The original document could be included in an Appendix.

If you're sure you want to attempt writing in dialect, you must read widely in the literature of the period to assimilate the assumptions, attitudes and turns of phrase of the age as well as its vocabulary. If you have already done this and have an exhaustive knowledge of the language of a particular region and period, it could well be a contribution to scholarship to summarise your findings in an Appendix.

On a practical level, unloading into the story too much undramatised research, however interesting in itself, will try your readers' patience. Similarly, most of us don't want to interrupt our reading to look up unusual words in a Glossary at the end of the book. Always keep in mind the educational level and tolerance of your target readership.

The next chapter has more on how — and whether — to include raw research data in your book.

Chapter 9:
Dealing with gaps and original documents
Getting from draft to finished manuscript

GAPS

When you feel you know nothing …

You may be anxious that there are gaps in your story
– that you simply can't find out *why* great-great-great-
uncle Job moved to Sussex. Creative writers have a
range of techniques for dealing with gaps and mysteries,
and the book that results is often the richer for it. As a
family historian, you included everything; creative
writing, by contrast, requires selection more than
inclusion

This chapter contains ideas for both papering over
the cracks and for highlighting – even celebrating –
those cracks. The first is not necessarily the better of
the two solutions.   Presenting the reader with an
enigma recognises the unfathomable nature of human
experience. It also invites readers to take a proactive
part in making sense of the material, trying to solve
the mystery.

There have been several celebrated biographies
where the biographer takes on the role of detective and
tries to piece together a book from flimsy and unreliable
evidence. A J A Symons, author of *The Quest For
Corvo,* set out to recover any known facts about the
mysterious writer Frederick William Rolfe (1860-1913)
who called himself Baron Corvo and fantasised about
suddenly being made Pope. His ramshackle life
involved financial catastrophe, homosexual romances

with boys and sleeping rough on a boat in Venice. After Rolfe's death, there was very little in the way of a paper-trail. Symons' book turns his hunt for missing details into a patient and absorbing quest with the reader, as it were, standing on the sidelines and cheering him on.

It took persistence for Ian Hamilton to embark on a biography of the notorious recluse J D Salinger, author of *The Catcher in the Rye*. Hamilton had some success with the 'living witness' approach, interviewing one of Salinger's former girlfriends, but *In Search of J D Salinger* is chiefly a meditation on the difficulty of writing biography when the biographee is unco-operative. Hamilton spares his readers nothing, even writing in his book that there were other people in America he might have interviewed but he couldn't afford the air-fare. The book's honesty is engaging. Most of us have an instinctive sympathy for the underdog.

The conclusion to draw is that even if you lack important evidence, a seemingly impossible task is still worth attempting as there is a story *in the very attempt*. Most family historians are not in such dire straits, luckily. The fact that you are reading this book indicates you have collected quantities of material and any remaining gaps will be easily finessed.

Amongst your raw material will be a plethora of dates, facts and statistics, but you may choose not to include them in the main text – or at all. There are worthy precedents for keeping facts *out* of creative non-fiction. Dickens experienced a sinking feeling when asked to write an article about Newgate Prison. His solution was to produce an impressionistic piece and warn the reader accordingly:

We have only to premise, that we do not intend to fatigue the reader with any statistical accounts of the prison; they will be found at length in numerous reports of numerous committees, and a variety of authorities of equal weight. We took no notes, made no memoranda, measured none of the yards, ascertained the exact number of inches in no particular room: are unable even to report of how many apartments the gaol is composed. We saw the prison, and saw the prisoners; and what we did see, and what we thought, we will tell at once in our own way. (from 'A Visit to Newgate' in *Sketches by Boz)*

Many of Dickens' readers must have been relieved, not affronted, that the investigator was giving a personal response rather than writing a government paper bloated with facts. You may wish to follow his lead, with or without placing a disclaimer at the start of your book.

When you know a lot but it's not joined up …

If your intention is to write, not a detective story but as full an account of your family as possible, you may still find puzzles of various kinds and want to resolve them. Where your research is patchy, like a collection of sharp snapshots with nothing joining them together, one way of ordering your material would be to present it as a series of linked short stories. Laurie Lee's autobiography *Cider With Rosie* is a collection of chapters devoted to a diversity of topics such as village festivals, the boy's glamorous uncles, the early life of his mother, village schools in rural England between the wars, and so on. The characters and setting remain the same for each chapter but the author's focus changes and apart from a reference to the end of the Great War, chronology is not emphasised.

You might also be inspired by Ronald Blythe's *Akenfield* based on oral history in Suffolk in the late 1960s. Villagers' monologues are linked by character sketches and interconnecting commentaries giving Blythe's own impressions of the area. These overlapping stories are orchestrated into a seamless garment, the village's history told by a chorus of different voices. *Akenfield* is teeming with ideas and inspiration for the family historian. In the case of your own project, there will be more emphasis on the 'longitudinal' picture: you will be systematically exploring the fortunes of a relatively small number of individuals (a family) over a period of time. Blythe's approach, by contrast, is 'latitudinal' – interviewing a wide range of people and recording historical data simply as it arose in the interviews.

Here are some ideas for unifying a diversity of stories from different generations of your family:

❑　Set the linked stories in a single geographical location – the same farm, town or region.
❑　Organise the plot round a vocation or trade practised by different generations of your family – mining, farming, teaching, nursing, the church, the armed forces, etc.
❑　Look at the lives of womenfolk in your family down the centuries.
❑　Examine what different marriages in different historical eras might have been like.
❑　Give symbolic meaning to some artefact – a

house or an heirloom, perhaps – which has been
passed down from family member to family
member.

❑ Look at family gravestones and epitaphs and use
these as a starting-point and a motif.

A venerable example of a book tracing the exercise
of a craft by a particular family is George Sturt's *The
Wheelwright's Shop*. Sturt covers the period 1706 to
1923 and the book coheres nicely round a locality and
the traditional craft pursued there. He includes
character sketches of the workmen, details of the
minutiae of their job, and a moving testimony to the
effect of a landscape on the men who work in it. The
age-old mystical link between land, trees, men and
horses is so powerfully drawn that chronology seems
almost irrelevant.

When you have a complete story but it's a bit 'thin'

In fiction, the writer often sets up a pattern by using
one character to 'mirror' the personality traits of the
protagonist, or a situation which throws into relief the
character's own predicament. You could enrich your
story's background, or fill in a gap, by referring to
contemporary figures whose lives resembled your
protagonist's or differed sharply from them. If your great-
grandmother was in domestic service, you could fill in
the plot by using other contemporary evidence of how
servants lived then. (See for example Hannah Cullwick's
diaries, mentioned in Select Bibliography.) Alternatively,
read Queen Victoria's diary for the same period and

contrast the life *she* led with the life of toil and humiliation experienced by your ancestor. Or do both.

This might be an occasion for introducing a sub-plot with marginal characters to keep readers interested and glide over any omissions in the main plot. Another technique is to create a collage of contemporary material, e.g. from newspapers, to present a 'slice of life' from the society your ancestors inhabited. Your Timeline will be invaluable here, placing your family's known history alongside significant national events, cultural trends, new books being published and music composed. Who was on the throne? What wars were being fought, Acts of Parliament being passed, new inventions being devised? For those not allergic to statistics, even these can be eloquent: to what extent was wealth distributed in that society, and to what extent did it remain in the hands of the few? How tall were working class boys compared to their more fortunate contemporaries born into middle class homes? How long did people live, on average?

As well as using verbatim quotes from contemporary documents, you could search for novelists' accounts of (say) someone getting married or witnessing a will. Stories can be filled out with invented direct speech, particularly if you have a gift for writing in the right 'period' style or dialect. You may feel especially close to one of your characters and able to invent an interior monologue expressing their secret thoughts in their own words.

If any of your ancestors were at a school that still exists, read the various school histories and try to reconstruct their lives as school-children. If that school is no longer in existence and no documents survive, find another school of the same type and read about what it was like during the relevant historical period. Perhaps a factory similar to the one your ancestor worked in has deposited records in the local museum or record office. If so, these could be plundered for atmosphere and period detail. If you can't find any historical evidence of this kind, turn to literature.

The location of your ancestors' homes may be rich in history and you could make your story reverberate by going back as far as you can and finding out what the life of medieval peasants in that area might have been like. There may be interesting customs, superstitions or folklore connected to that area in days gone by. Or was it, perhaps, the scene of a particularly sensational crime?

More modestly, you could discuss what was in the news, what songs were popular, what fashions were all the rage, when one of your characters was born or died. This is an effortless and appealing way of creating a context that your readers can relate to. The absence of minor facts about your ancestors will not bother your readers as the details of daily life in times gone by are so enthralling.

You will need to make sure that any background information is fully integrated into your book. If you decide to place your family against a background of national history, think through the relevance of this history to your own family. A vigorous debate is taking place in academia at present about the validity of 'periodisation', i.e. dividing history into named chunks and applying these categories to the culture and literature of the past in an attempt to illuminate them. If your antecedents were marginalised in any way – by

gender, poverty, living in remote rural areas, etc. –
metropolitan trends might have had little bearing on
their lives. Such cultural revolutions as the Romantic
Movement or the Naughty Nineties would have passed
unnoticed by an illiterate agricultural labourer of the
nineteenth century.

When you know what to say but don't want to get sued …

There could even be legal reasons for withholding
information that you have acquired (see Legal Matters
in the next chapter). Although the dead cannot sue,
their surviving family are entitled to if the facts you
uncover and publicise have implications for them. Even
if you are legally in the clear, you will probably wish to
avoid distressing the living descendants of one of your
'characters'. For reasons of sensitivity and law, it is
probably best to exercise tact and exclude certain tit-
bits. You can always drop hints about them!

The next decision to make is whether you are going
to inform the reader of an omission or gloss over it. If
you choose to glide over a lacuna in this way, several
suggestions are given above for distracting the reader's
attention so that missing material goes unnoticed. If
you are going to highlight the absence, a very brief
unapologetic explanation is sufficient unless the
problem is part of a larger mystery and you want to
enhance the element of 'quest' in your book.

To sum up: gaps, alternative versions and apparent
contradictions can be stimulating for your readers.
They don't have to be an obstacle to putting together a

convincing page-turner of a book. Handled sensitively and with literary flair, enigmas can emphasise the mysterious nature of life, showing that we can *never* finally know everything, and there are always multiple stories and interpretations, even when we apparently have all the facts.

ORIGINAL DOCUMENTS

It is advisable to keep the tone of your book consistent throughout, or your readers will become disorientated. For this reason, I recommend limiting quotations to a maximum of a page, or about 400 words. Anything longer than this which can't be abbreviated or broken up with editorial comment is best placed in an Appendix at the back of the book, quite separate from your main text. Unless you are brave enough to compile an experimental biography with quantities of documents for your readers to interpret, your role as author is to select telling details and point up their significance, either through explicit comment or artful juxtaposition.

We have already noted that some biographers make a virtue out of presenting 'raw' data, but this is a risky strategy for a novice writer. At worst, you could you lose control altogether and present readers with a confusing mass of material and no way to evaluate it. For most of us, the best solution is to process and shape the main text of your book and relegate awkward research data and documents such as wills, inventories and letters to the endmatter.

Endmatter

'Endmatter' is the publishing term for supporting material which appears at the very end of a book, such as the bibliography, the index and any appendices. Appendices enable you to preserve and publish valuable data without having to manhandle large documents into the main text, where they will struggle to break free of any pattern or theme you are trying to impose on your family's story.

How much of your original research should you preserve for posterity in the endmatter of your book, rather than trying to force it into the main text? If you examine your List of Events/Storyline, you may decide to put some of the following in the endmatter:

❑ legal documents, e.g. wills and inventories
❑ diagrams and plans
❑ samples of handwriting
❑ chronology showing historical events in relation to your family's progress
❑ maps of locations where action takes place
❑ source details, in form of Notes relating to the main text
❑ acknowledgements
❑ picture credits, acknowledging the source of any illustrations
❑ bibliography
❑ glossary of words (trade terms, dialect forms, etc.)

WORD PERFECT: GETTING FROM DRAFT TO FINISHED MANUSCRIPT

If you have followed the advice in chapter 1, you will have produced a complete rough draft of your book which will need several revisions before it is ready for the press. To add to your research and writing skills, you are now going to practise editing your own work. This process is of course a great deal easier if you have typed the book on to a computer and can alter a word or sentence here and there without needing to rewrite the whole page. But if you are not computer-literate and have written your book on loose sheets of lined paper, don't despair. It's slower to revise a hand-written draft than a word-processed draft, but if you are determined to see your book finished, you will do it. Don't forget Tolstoy wrote *War and Peace* by hand!

Most writers produce many drafts of a book before they are finally satisfied, and in most cases the later versions of the book will be shorter and 'tighter' than the first and second attempts. Give yourself a break of at least a week between finishing the first draft and starting the revision. When you take your draft out of a drawer again, it will read like someone else's work and you will have the objectivity to detect any faults.

1. Read the entire draft through quickly and strike out (a) waffle, that doesn't add to the story, and (b) any fancy 'purple passages' that don't match the overall tone of the book. You should be able to reduce the word-count by at least 10-15% in this first read-through.

2. Next, read it again from the start to get a sense of the shape of the book. Are incidents related in the best possible order and does the story 'flow' nicely from one episode to the next? Have you inadvertently repeated an anecdote? Does a passage need to come out altogether, to be published separately as a magazine article? This stage may involve extensive re-writing and some material will be discarded altogether, but don't put it in the bin just yet. If you are typing on a computer, give each draft a unique name (e.g. the date when you finished it) and keep these files on floppy disks in a drawer to avoid confusion with the current draft. If you are writing by hand, place unwanted material in a box-file marked 'dustbin' and write on the notes the date you discarded them and why.

3. Once you have cleared up any anomalies in the structure, read the book aloud to yourself and underline as you go along any awkward, ambiguous or clumsy phrasing. Then go back and improve the style of the passages you have marked.

4. Hand your draft to a friend you respect and ask him or her to read it *critically*, with the express intention of seeking out mistakes and faults. It is painful to have your work criticised, but an objective response from a sensible person will save you heart-ache and expense at the next stage — getting your book into print.

Chapter 10: Into print –
publishing and self-publishing

So far, this book has concentrated on the *process* of writing. Now it's time to look at the *product* – your finished book and how you will get it to your readership. First, using commercial publishers.

THE ESSENTIALS OF GETTING PUBLISHED

At the time of writing there are around 1,800 publishers in the UK but many form part of giant multi-national conglomerates. The large publishing houses receive thousands of unsolicited manuscripts every year and it is estimated that under 0.5% of this total is accepted for publication. Simply opening, reading and returning these submissions creates a great deal of work for publishers. Would-be authors must approach publishers in a professional manner if they want to be taken seriously and not dismissed as a nuisance.

ESSENTIAL: Steep yourself in the pages of a recent copy of the *Writers' & Artists' Yearbook* (see Select Bibliography). Every library service will have at least one copy of this reference book. Read very closely the entries listing details of publishers you might contact and follow their instructions scrupulously. It is pointless sending a biography to a publisher who clearly states in the *Yearbook* 'poetry only'.

ESSENTIAL: Present your submission in a way that meets the target publisher's criteria. Some publishers include submission guidelines in their *Yearbook* entry or their own web site. Generally speaking, when approaching a publisher you should not at first send your whole book: a synopsis and one sample chapter is usually sufficient.

ESSENTIAL: Your manuscript must be typed/word-processed. If you can't type yourself, telephone the human resources department of your local college, university or hospital and ask if you may place a card on the staff notice-board. A briefly worded card with your telephone number will attract several enquiries as most secretaries are only too pleased to earn money in the evenings typing something as interesting as a book. Modern word-processing packages include a word-count facility, so offer a rate per thousand words and pay the typist when she has finished and done a word-count. You can establish the going rate for your part of the country by ringing up a typing bureau listed in Yellow Pages and asking what they charge per thousand words.

ESSENTIAL: You must include a stamped addressed envelope with your submission. If you want your synopsis and sample chapter back, weigh them carefully and make sure you send an envelope large enough and with the correct postage for return. If your book is saved on a computer and you don't need the sample back, type at the top of your covering letter 'Return Not Requested' and simply send an ordinary-sized envelope with standard postage so the publisher can write back to you to state whether your manuscript is of interest or not.

LAYOUT ESSENTIALS
- ❏ Manuscripts must be double-spaced and printed on one side of the paper only. If you indent the first line of paragraphs, there is no need to leave

another space between paragraphs. Leave 1½ inches for the left-hand margin, one inch for right hand margin and two inches for top and bottom of the page. Do not 'justify' the type, to make a straight right-hand margin, but leave it 'aligned left' so that individual letters are evenly spaced. Use ordinary white paper and do not decorate it with clip-art pictures as this looks frivolous.

❏ Keep your synopsis and sample chapter on loose sheets; do not bind them in any way (staples, ring-binders, separate chapters in plastic pockets, etc). Simply place the loose sheets inside a manila folder and write your name and the book's title on a white label stuck to it. It is acceptable to put your name and address as well as title of the book on the top right-hand corner of every page in small type. This is easy to do on word-processing packages using a 'header'. Pages must be numbered in case they are dropped in the publisher's office and get out of order.

❏ Enclose your synopsis and sample chapter with a business-like covering letter and a brief biographical sketch of yourself on a separate sheet. Don't ask publishers for their advice and comments; they simply haven't time and the request will make you look unprofessional.

To sum up, your initial proposal to target publishers should include:

1. A4 typed covering letter in impeccable business English
2. A4 typed biographical sketch of author
3. A4 typed synopsis/summary of your book – one page is usually sufficient
4. A sample chapter, typed, double-spaced with wide margins, the title and your name and page number on every page
5. A large or small stamped addressed envelope, depending on whether you want your submission back

Because of the sheer bulk of unsolicited manuscripts, many publishers have begun to stipulate 'no un-agented submissions'. This means you cannot approach those publishers direct but must first get on the books of a literary agent and the agent then approaches publishers on your behalf. The advantage of using agents is that they know the publishing industry, will send out your manuscript only to likely publishers and will not charge you anything up-front. Regrettably, agents have limited capacity for taking on new authors, so you have to pass through *their* filtering system before you're accepted and then they still have to find your book a publisher. It is not guaranteed. When you are published, they will charge you a percentage (around 15%) of your gross income from the book.

There are lists of agents in the *Writers' & Artists' Yearbook* and, as with publishers, you should contact only those who specialise in your type of book. Your query letter should describe your book briefly and ask the literary agent if they will look at it. If they agree, send it off together with return postage. Don't give up if, after several tries, no agent will place you on their books. There are still some publishers who will look at 'un-agented' submissions, and if you do end up famous, agents will beat a path to your door.

A word of warning: you should never go to a publisher's or agent's office unless invited to do so, and keep telephoning to an absolute minimum. Publishers are simply too busy to cope with hundreds of authors (and freelance editors, indexers, designers, illustrators, printers, etc.) all of whom think they are special. Try to be considerate.

Authors' Royalties

Authors automatically own the copyright to their own works and they license this to the publisher, who pays them royalties of a certain percentage of the price of the book. Because of massive discounting by bookshops and supermarkets, it is more and more common for the percentage to be of the *net* price received by the publisher after deduction of booksellers' discount. The publisher makes up the accounts six months after publication of the book, and then there is likely to be a further delay before the author receives his or her first royalties cheque. Some publishers (not all) pay the author an 'advance' on royalties, though the huge advances you read about in the newspapers are abnormal and are paid to only a handful of writers.

Most published authors do not sell enough copies of their books to make a living from royalties alone. Research by Nielsen BookScan found that in 2004, only 2% of the 1.2 million titles sold in the UK achieved sales of more than 5,000 copies. After your publisher has granted discounts to bookshops, the author of a paperback edition might receive only 50p per book, and 5,000 x 50p only comes to £2,500. You need a trickle of royalties from several books before earnings become significant. However, being a published author can open up other avenues, such as invitations to give talks and lectures.

Getting articles published in magazines

As well as publishing your research in book form, you could also sell your material to suitable magazines and journals as a series of articles. Typically, magazines want articles of 1000-1500 words and you can find their Contributors' Guidelines on the magazine's web site, or alternatively write in (enclosing an s.a.e.) and request them.

You might, for example, write a series about the different generations of your family; about the trades they were engaged in; about the different regions of the country they were associated with, in times gone by; or even link your family to a significant anniversary. Payment is often notional, with some journals 'paying' their contributors with six copies of the journal to give to friends. This is not to be despised, however, as having an article published in a magazine is proof that your writing deserves a wider audience. This will add to your credibility when you write to publishers.

Exercises in nostalgia are comforting and enjoyable to large sectors of the population and you may well have uncovered material in your family research that could be written up appropriately. There are several successful magazines catering for the heritage and nostalgia market. Buy or borrow some of these, read them closely to absorb the preferred style, then send a query letter to the editor asking if the magazine would be interested in an article on X. Make your query letter brief almost to the point of brusqueness and include an s.a.e. in the hope of getting a reply. This is not guaranteed.

Magazine editors are even busier than book publishers and you won't make a good impression by being elaborately polite or waffling on irrelevantly. Keep to the point. At this stage, it's not necessary to send samples of your writing, but if you already have other publications to your name, list these briefly. Legally, what you are offering the magazine is F.B.S.R. (First British Serial Rights) in your proposed article.

SELF-PUBLISHING

Submitting books to publishers typically involves 40 rejections and a two or three year wait, even for those who are in the end successful. It is hardly surprising that more and more authors are turning to self-publishing.

Over the last 20 years, it has become much cheaper to get a book produced. Typesetting costs are reduced by using computer programs and very small print-runs can 'break even', or even make a small profit, if the target market for a book is carefully defined.

Self-publishers occasionally find that after they have published their book, commercial publishers begin to take a belated interest. There are three reasons for this:

1. By publishing the book yourself and making a go of it, you have tested the market and the commercial publisher is taking less of a risk.

2. Having marketed your own book, you have proved you understand the business side of publishing and can be trusted to be co-operative and proactive in getting books into bookshops.

3. Your success can be celebrated by the media in a ready-made slot reserved for 'success of the underdog' stories – downtrodden self-published author makes good.

It's not very convincing for Mary Brown to sell her own book through Mary Brown Publishing so think of a different name for your publishing imprint. The Companies House web site lists all the names of existing limited companies, so you can avoid using these names, although it does not cover businesses which are partnerships or sole traders. You should also explore the internet, searching for your proposed name with '.com' or '.co.uk' or '.org' or '.net' (etc.) as a suffix. Once you are reasonably confident no other publisher has already chosen your proposed business name, set up a bank or building society account in that name.

Bear in mind that by selling books through your own publishing imprint, you will be generating a income that HM Revenue and Customs may be interested in. You will need to keep accurate and exhaustive records.

If you have not attempted an enterprise like this before, it's time to take stock of your talents, experiences, contacts and inner resources and relate these to the bookselling market. Ask yourself:

- ❑ WHO do you know? Societies you belong to, and magazines you subscribe to may be interested in your book. Write something for the letters page about your proposed book, offer an interview or short article. Do you know any experts who might write the foreword or promote your book among their peers? Are you friendly with your local book-shop (for a book-launch) or printer (for free advice, and agreement to pay in instalments)?

- ❑ WHAT do you know? Can you type and use the internet? Could you learn typesetting? Do you have a flair for design which will enable you to set out the book in an eye-catching way? Have you investigated building a web site to publicise your book?

- ❑ WHAT'S THE MARKET LIKE? Are there any other books like yours? Does your book have a particular slant on a popular subject, which will enable you to target a clear and discrete readership?

You will of course need to set aside time, space, money and energy for office chores. But the main challenges for self-publishers are (a) paying the printer's bill, as you usually need to settle this long before you receive any revenue from sales, and (b) organising marketing and distribution.

Subscription publishing

One way of raising the money to print your book is through soliciting subscriptions from interested parties, for example, people with the same surname as you who might be interested in reading about your branch of the family. You could advertise in an appropriate magazine and journal or contact likely parties direct, by letter or email. (As always, make sure you observe the principles of Data Protection.) Your approach to would-be subscribers should outline your book in as much detail as possible and set a price per copy based on the print quotes you have obtained. Subscribers will enjoy seeing their names in your book when it appears, so reserve a page or two to list their names and thank them for their support. Your leaflet should mention a closing date for this offer so there is a point at which you can safely sit down and assess how successful you have been. Asking for subscriptions is a relatively low-cost exercise. If interest is insufficient, you can always send any monies back before printing the book, then go on to explore other avenues.

And in case anyone thinks this is demeaning, remember that many landmarks of literature appeared only through the kindness of patrons and subscribers: the first edition of Milton's *Paradise Lost,* perhaps the greatest epic poem in English, was financed by subscription. You are in good company.

Legal matters

In addition to the legal constraints on *any* business or freelance work (e.g. the obligation to keep records and observe the Data Protection Act), there are specific regulations relevant to publishing and marketing books.

LEGAL DEPOSIT: You are required by law to deposit six copies of your title, within a month of its publication, to certain national and university libraries. One copy should be sent to the British Library (or the Irish Copyright Agency if appropriate) and five copies to the Copyright Libraries Agency. See Useful Addresses at the end of this book for contact details.

COPYRIGHT: If you plan to quote from other books, or use photographs you did not take yourself, it is important to be clear about copyright. The main legislation is the Copyright, Designs and Patents Act 1988 as modified by the Duration of Copyright and Rights in Performance Regulations 1995. In brief, copyright is effective for 70 years after a book's publication or 70 years after the author's death, whichever is the later. That is, if an author died in 1930, his work *may* be out of copyright by the year 2001. However, if some of his work was first published posthumously, the copyright in those works persists until 70 years after the date of publication. The rules governing photographs are even more complicated as any people depicted in the photographs may retain rights over the use of their image.

PERMISSIONS: If you are sure the work you are quoting from is still in copyright, you need to find who currently holds the copyright and obtain permission to quote. Ensure you apply for permission to the original publisher. A paperback edition may have been published by another firm, but you need to write to the publisher of the original hardback volume. Start the process of permission-seeking as soon as you know you wish to quote substantially from a copyright publication. You may be redirected to other publishers and will often have to send reminders. Keep records of everything you do to trace the copyright owner(s) and compose a disclaimer for the book stating that investigations have been undertaken but if any copyright holders have been inadvertently overlooked, they should get in touch and the deficiency will be repaired in future editions.

If you wish to quote from family documents, always get permission in writing from relevant family members. Even a spiral-bound publication with a print-run of 100 counts as publishing so the laws of copyright and libel still apply.

FAIR DEALING: Luckily, there is a legal provision called 'Fair Dealing' which removes some of these formalities for brief quotations. Under the Copyright Designs and Patents Act 1988, you are allowed to quote from books for the purpose of criticism or review. It is still wise to apply for permission if you are using extracts of more than 400 words, or a couple of lines from a song or poem.

PLAGIARISM: This word derives from a Latin term meaning 'kidnapping'. It is the offence of dishonestly using another author's writing in a book with your name on the cover. Writers have unwittingly committed plagiarism by not keeping their research notes properly organised and annotated. As you gather quotations together to appear in your finished book, make sure you identify them to yourself as quotations, e.g. by placing them in quotation marks with the author's name in brackets at the end to remind you. It is all too easy to forget where you found a particular sentence and include it in your book without acknowledgement, giving the impression that you wrote it yourself. Most of us have no such evil intentions but carelessness can be dangerous.

LIBEL: Libel is printing false remarks about a living person that damages their reputation in the eyes of right-thinking people. Changing the names of individuals is not enough to protect you from a libel action. Although the dead cannot sue, statements about deceased people have implications for the living. For example, if you discovered that your great-grandparents weren't married, or that your great-grandfather had a mental illness, subsequent generations may not want this publicised. Writers have a duty to the living, to the dead, and to the truth. Sometimes you have to make difficult moral judgements and no two writers will come up with exactly the same solution faced with a certain dilemma.

ISBNs and BAR CODES: Although it is not a legal requirement to provide your book with an ISBN (International Standard Book Number), and you will save yourself money if you don't, it makes ordering by bookshops and libraries so much easier that anyone seeking a wide market for their book should apply for an ISBN. At present these have ten digits; future ISBNs will have thirteen. The ISBN Agency will advise you on everything to do with ISBNs: see Useful Addresses at the end of this book. Booksellers and their wholesalers are increasingly demanding bar codes on the cover of books. These can be purchased from companies on the internet and some printers will source and place bar codes for you: ask the price before you agree to this service. Once you have obtained an ISBN for your book, the next step is to fill in a Nielsen BookData new title form to notify the book trade of your new title. The ISBN Agency supply these forms on request, or you can complete a form on-line.

PUBLIC LENDING RIGHT: If you are very optimistic about your book's appeal, you can register your details with the Public Lending Right Office as soon as book is published. You will earn a few pence per loan from a public library – 5.26p at the time of writing (late 2005) but this figure is reviewed annually at the end of December. The registration process is simple and the address to write to can be found in Useful Addresses at the end of this book.

Editing, designing and printing your book

If your book is still in handwritten form, now is the time to get it typed up on a word-processor. You will need to devise your own 'house style' to ensure your book is not only grammatically correct but that the style is consistent throughout. The *Oxford Guide to Style,* edited by Robert Ritter (see Select Bibliography), offers much detailed advice.

Footnotes at the bottom of a page are difficult to typeset as a small change in a footnote can throw out the alignment of dozens of pages. It is best to avoid footnotes altogether and either find a way to work the material into the main text, or use endnotes collected together at the end of your book.

Once your book has been typed in a common word-processing format, any printer will be able to handle it. The printer's task is to transfer your word-processed text into a desk-top publishing file (e.g. Ventura, Quark

XPress or Pagemaker format) from which your book will be printed. Your printer will advise you on the pros and cons of different book sizes.

If you anticipate most of your sales will be by mail-order, consider a format that will be easy and cheap to post. A modest paperback volume could be sent out in stout C5 envelopes (115g manila basket-weave) reinforced with cardboard from boxes available free at the supermarket. If origami is not your strong point, a small book could be enclosed in bubblewrap and popped inside a C5 reinforced envelope which has cardboard on one face and 'Please do not bend' printed on the front.

To get best value from the printer's paper, the number of pages in your book should ideally be a multiple of 32. Using the most popular weights of paper, your book needs to be at least 64 pages long to make a spine thick enough to carry a title. Without a visible title on the spine, your book will simply 'disappear' on book-shop and library shelves. Remind the printer that you want the text on the spine to be legible when the book is placed flat with the *upper* panel visible.

It is worth obtaining a number of print quotes from different printing firms and asking the printers further questions so that the quotations you receive are comparable and reflect exactly what you want. A printer may carry out most functions of book production (origination, plate-making, collating, binding, printing) on his own premises, or he may subcontract some tasks to outside specialists. If a printer's bill looks too large, ask him to break it down into its separate components. You may be able to negotiate on one of the stages of the process and get the price down.

Once you've chosen your printer, send him an order in writing covering the following points:

- ❑ Today's date; your name, address, email address if applicable, and telephone number; delivery address if different.
- ❑ Size of book (e.g. Royal Octavo, A-format paperback, etc.); number of pages; type and colour of paper; colour of print (usually black).
- ❑ Type and weight of card to be used for cover; type of binding; number of colours to be used on cover; whether cover is to be laminated; whether you want spare copies of the cover for publicity purposes.
- ❑ Illustrations; any services you expect printer to undertake in improving the artwork.
- ❑ Whether the printer is obtaining a bar-code for you and whether there an additional cost for this.
- ❑ How many copies you want printed.
- ❑ If you state, 'Proofs must be submitted before binding', you have an opportunity to spot and correct mistakes. Your printer may add an extra charge for proofs.

Price

If you are planning to sell your book through retail outlets, add together your costs and divide by the number you plan to print (less any free copies to be given away for review). Retail prices used to be calculated at around four or five times the cost per unit, so if the book cost £2.50 to print and market, the cover price was set at £9.99 or more. However, with wholesalers demanding 55% discount, this formula is no longer a reliable rule of thumb and every book needs to be assessed individually in relation to (a) current conditions in the book trade, and (b) the cost of marketing the book, which can be considerable. There is more on marketing later in this chapter.

Selling direct to the customer by mail order, rather than through the book trade, makes it possible to have a selling price much closer to the production cost. There is no obligation to print a price on the cover of a book: leaving the price off gives you the freedom to tailor the price to individual markets. However, if this is your choice, you will need to make sure your bar code does not have a price embedded in it.

Final thoughts on self-publishing

The expenditure of time, money and effort involved in self-publishing your book can be considerable and it is wise to quantify at the start the outlay of money and time you need to devote to this enterprise. Tasks and costs include:

❑ Registering for a block of ISBNs (you can't buy just one)
❑ Opening a bank account in the name of your publishing imprint
❑ Costs involved in researching the market for your book
❑ Pre-publication publicity costs
❑ Cost of setting up a web site, if you want an internet presence
❑ Origination – preparation of text for printing

- ❑ Printing and binding costs, including any delivery charges
- ❑ Packing and posting review copies and press releases
- ❑ Posting six free copies for Legal Deposit purposes
- ❑ Cost of printing advertising leaflets/order forms
- ❑ Cost of posting leaflets/order forms to journals and societies
- ❑ Cost of packing and posting the book to your customers

Put like this, it is a little daunting and you may be tempted to contact those companies that advertise in newspapers and magazines for authors. Beware. These are often vanity publishers who prey on people who don't understand how publishing works. Reputable publishers never advertise for authors: they are already swamped with unsolicited manuscripts. Vanity publishers typically take substantial sums of money from writers, contract to print large numbers of books but only bind a few of them. They have no distribution whatsoever and an author will sell no books through these companies. Bookshops recognise vanity imprints and will not waste shelf space on them. Worse still, some of these firms are so badly run that they have a tendency to go out of business before producing anything at all for their customers.

There are several good magazines on the market specifically for writers (details are given at the back of this book) and these carry advertisements from companies offering to facilitate the process of *self-publishing.* This is a more transparent and honest approach and it would not hurt to ask for these companies' brochures. The fact remains, however, that anyone capable of researching their family's history is capable of writing a book; and anyone capable of writing a book is capable of publishing it themselves. It only takes a further application of the common sense, hard work and good judgement you have already shown you have.

MARKETING YOUR BOOK

Marketing through magazines and societies

Marketing is the key to making a success of small print runs, and once again family historians are in a privileged position. There are many magazines, societies and web sites in Britain and abroad where you can publicise and sell your book to like-minded individuals.

In addition to fellow family historians, your book may appeal to hobbyists, many of whom have their own magazines and membership lists. For example, if your great-grandfather worked on the railways, steam railway societies might agree to send out a leaflet with their regular mailings to members.

Again, there could be a *geographically* distinct market for your book if your family was associated with a town, village or region of the country. If this is the case do some market research before finishing the writing and getting print quotes. Will local residents be willing to pay £10 maximum or only £2? Should the book be nostalgic or scholarly? Then work out how many households there are in that district (not individuals: households) and assume 10% of households can be persuaded to buy your book. Local libraries might buy a handful of copies and the local newspaper will appreciate a free copy for review.

Some advertising copy-writing will be called for, and you can start practising this by writing the 'blurb' for the back of your book. The selling points you highlight in the blurb must be directly relevant to the market you are targeting. If you scan through the paperbacks in your local bookshop, you will find publishers often use a three-part formula: (a) a striking first sentence, often printed in bold type, making the reader want to know more, (b) a paragraph giving more details about the contents of the book, (c) a final paragraph summing up the benefits for the audience you are targeting, e.g. 'a must for medieval historians!' This blurb can then be used as the basis for classified advertisements in specialist magazines, leaflets distributed through family history societies, and so forth.

Send out review copies to any relevant journals or societies that have newsletters. *Willings Press Guide*, available in reference libraries, lists all UK periodicals. You can also hunt them down on the internet or refer to the *Writers' and Artists' Yearbook*. If you are the outgoing type, write a press release and send it to newspapers and the broadcasting media. There are a number of excellent 'how to' books on the market about writing press releases; you local library will have one. Local radio stations have many hours of broadcasting time to fill and an interesting press release may lead to an invitation to talk on the radio. The presenter and his staff will bend over backwards to put you at your ease and broadcasting credentials will give you credibility when you market your book to shops and societies.

The cost of mailing exploratory letters to special interest societies can be substantial. First, they will expect to see a copy of the leaflet you wish them to distribute, so you will need to get a leaflet designed and printed. If you do not have the computer skills to do this yourself, the costs are likely to amount to £40 for origination of leaflet + around £100 for printing 10,000 A5 leaflets. And yes, you will need at least 10,000 if you are serious about selling a few hundred books by mail order. Then, someone needs to type an appropriate letter to an officer of the society, consuming time, ink and paper. Then you'll need to buy stamps. Not all the societies you write to will reply.

Societies who respond may levy a charge for distributing an advertising flyer, but will be eager to have a free review copy. It is advisable to make a telephone call to get the name and address of their reviewer (or editor of the journal if appropriate). Then send out your book with a review slip describing the book as follows:

- ❑ Title
- ❑ Author
- ❑ Publisher
- ❑ ISBN
- ❑ Price
- ❑ Size (format and measurements in millimetres)
- ❑ Extent (number of pages)
- ❑ Illustrations
- ❑ Binding (e.g. paperback, laminated cover)
- ❑ Publication date
- ❑ Ordering details (e.g. 'direct from publisher')

Retail sales

Most novice authors expect to see their books in bookshops. However, because of the bookseller's discount, it is very hard to make a profit from bookshop sales and you would need to be your own 'sales rep' and trail round a large number of shops. It is possible to find a firm of distributors who will represent a one-book publisher, but they will expect a proportion of sales income (around 20%) as their commission, eating into your tiny profit margin. Booksellers expect at least 35% discount and they traditionally benefit from free carriage or postage – i.e. *you* have to bear the cost of getting the books to them. Book-shops and wholesalers may want to negotiate even larger discounts (40-55% is not unusual), and the big chains will have set the discount centrally, so it is a waste of time trying to negotiate with individual shops.

Heavy booksellers' discounts plus distributor's commission mean that family biographies are best marketed through societies and magazines, then sold via mail order. You still need an ISBN and a bar code, however, as enthusiasts who read a review of your book and want to buy it may well ask their local bookshop to order a copy, and you would lose these orders if the lack of an ISBN or bar code made ordering your book difficult for the bookseller.

While you are mulling over the business aspects of becoming a published author, why not exercise your creative side by attempting some of the imaginative tasks in the next chapter? Good practice for writing to publishers, composing blurbs, leaflets, press releases and the like.

Chapter 11: Limbering up –
simple creative writing exercises

Getting permission to quote verbatim from other books is time-consuming and expensive, so learning to write effectively will save you money. It will also take you on a journey of self-discovery.

First you need to develop an insatiable curiosity about words. Words are, after all, the writer's stock in trade. Buy a comprehensive dictionary and dip into it whenever you hear an unfamiliar word and wonder, 'Where did that come from?' A good dictionary will always give you the etymology of a word - some indication of its origin and the history of its use - and this can be profoundly revealing. Did you know that 'sarcasm' comes from a Greek expression meaning 'the tearing of flesh'? That a Victorian music hall song is commemorated for all time in the word 'jingoism'? Other interesting words to look up are radar, oxymoron, autopsy, dilapidated, simony and buxom.

In researching your family history, you developed an enquiring mind, resilience and persistence. To this repertoire, you now need to add observational skills. As a writer, you must be receptive to:

❑ words and their subtle shades of meaning
❑ the outside world
❑ yourself and your values
❑ other people
❑ books and other works of art

This sensitivity can be developed by keeping a journal in which to record miscellaneous thoughts and observations. Television presenter Michael Palin has kept a diary since 1969 and explained in a recent interview, 'Keeping a diary is like a daily jab with a pointed stick. It forces you to concentrate on life.' Your journal, like Palin's diary, is not only a mine of raw material that you can plunder for projects such as your family story, it is also a vital element of your training as a writer. Think of it as 'pre-writing'.

The Creative Process

You might not have tried creative writing since schooldays, but human beings are creative animals and it will soon come back to you. The first step is buying a notebook to use as your journal. A writer's journal is a 'rough book' in which you jot down anything that catches your eye. Keep a pocket-sized notebook with you at all times and scribble down anything surprising, beautiful, funny or strange that you see or hear. Your journal is private, so there is nothing that can't go in. The different entries don't even have to be related in any obvious way. Your journal entries might include:

- ❑ random observations on life
- ❑ reflections on your relationships with other people
- ❑ analysis of your own thoughts, feelings and personality
- ❑ your hopes and aspirations for the future
- ❑ memories of the past
- ❑ character sketches of people you know, or of strangers seen on a train

- ❑ conversations or puzzling fragments of dialogue
- ❑ anecdotes, funny incidents and stories
- ❑ ideas and inventions
- ❑ lists of things you like and dislike
- ❑ letters to people, alive and dead
- ❑ your experiences, good and bad
- ❑ descriptions of works of art - paintings, concerts, plays on TV, etc.
- ❑ nature and the weather
- ❑ important anniversaries
- ❑ interesting or sad places

Simple Exercises in Autobiographical Writing

If all this sounds a bit amorphous, start with some autobiographical writing. Just as no-one would run a marathon without first doing a great deal of training, so you need to 'limber up' for your book by practising writing about things you know. Simple exercises, quite separate from your family story, can build your confidence by demonstrating that you *can* do it. There is nothing mysterious or magical about being a writer. It is a craft like any other. All you need is some paper, a pen, a quiet place to write in and some time set aside to do it.

Your first exercises should be on topics very close to you, as the facts will be at your fingertips and you can concentrate all your energies on putting them into words. Take a pad of A4 lined paper and write one page on each of the following:

- ❑ A list of all the things, however small, that give you pleasure

- Who has annoyed you lately? Answer them back.
- List (a) your achievements, then (b) your feelings about these achievements. Then (c) analyse the system of values that makes these achievements significant for you. For example, you may have defied the local council over a proposed new building on a green field site. If you are proud of this, it shows you are someone who believes in standing up for him- or herself and someone who cares about the community and the environment.
- What is your most embarrassing memory? Write this down, in detail, even if you have to tear the sheet up afterwards.
- Think of a big change you have made (voluntarily) in your life. Was it motivated by trying to get *away* from something or by wanting to move *towards* something?
- Analyse what you enjoy reading. The things you read, and the ideas that excite you, define who you are and where you want to go in life. Reading is not passive, like watching TV, but active and creative: we have to imagine scenes and people based on descriptions made out of words.
- Without checking, what do you think is in your dustbin? If you disappeared and a policeman sorted through it for clues, what kind of a person would he conclude that you are?
- What if you'd made a different choice at a crucial crossroads in your life? Write your alternative life story.

Students on creative writing courses are often surprised at what they discover through autobiographical writing. You may also find that expressing yourself in private like this is quite therapeutic. By taking a writer's journal out and about with you, and watching other people closely, you will also begin to develop the capacity to imagine others' lives – vital if you are going to write your family's story.

*

Biographer Richard Holmes once wrote that 'The dead call to us out of the past. They ask to be heard, remembered, understood.' Biography-writing is a noble calling as well as being deeply fulfilling for the author. I hope that you enjoy writing your book as much as I have enjoyed writing this one.

SELECT BIBLIOGRAPHY

On the craft of biography

Gittings, Robert *The Nature of Biography*
(Heinemann, 1978)

Hamilton, Ian *Keepers of the Flame: Literary
Estates and the Rise of Biography*
(Hutchinson, 1992)

Holmes, Richard *Footsteps: Adventures of a
Romantic Biographer* (Hodder & Stoughton, 1985)

Holmes, Richard *Dr Johnson & Mr Savage*
(Hodder & Stoughton, 1993)

Holroyd, Michael *Works on Paper*
(Little, Brown, 2002)

Other titles of relevance to family biography

Ackerley, J R, *My Father and Myself*
(Bodley Head, 1968)

Blythe, Ronald *Akenfield* (Allen Lane, 1969)

Coe, Jonathan *Like a Fiery Elephant: the story of B
S Johnson* (Picador, 2004)

Gosse, Edmund *Father and Son: a study of two
temperaments* (Heinemann, 1907)

Hamilton, Ian *In Search of J D Salinger*
(Heinemann, 1988)

Lee, Laurie *Cider With Rosie*
(Hogarth Press, 1959)

Mallon, Thomas *A Book of One's Own: People and
their Diaries*
(Ticknor & Fields, 1984)

McCourt, Frank *Angela's Ashes*
(HarperCollins, 1996)

Raban, Jonathan *Coasting*
(Collins Harvill, 1986)

Stanley, Liz *The Diaries of Hannah Cullwick,
Victorian Maidservant*
(Virago, 1984)

Sturt, George *The Wheelwright's Shop*
(Cambridge University Press, 1923)

Symons, A J A *The Quest for Corvo: an
Experiment in Biography*
(Cassell, 1934)

Woodham-Smith, Cecil *The Reason Why*
(Constable, 1953)

Writing and publishing

Hoffman, Ann *Research for Writers*
(A & C Black, 7th edition, 2003)

Ritter, Robert *Oxford Guide to Style*
(Oxford University Press, 2002)

Turner, Barry (ed.) *The Writer's Handbook*
(Macmillan, published annually)

Writers' & Artists' Yearbook
(A & C Black, published annually)

MAGAZINES AND OTHER RESOURCES

The Bookseller: weekly trade magazine, available in libraries

Writers' Forum, Writing Magazine, Writers' News, and *Mslexia* are periodicals aimed at writers who are serious about their craft and about getting published. *Mslexia* only accepts submissions from women but contains articles that are equally of interest to a male readership. All four magazines can be ordered by subscription or through your newsagent.

Family Tree Magazine and *Practical Family History* are available at most newsagents or can be obtained direct from the publishers at 61 Great Whyte, Ramsey, Huntingdon, PE26 1HJ, United Kingdom. www.family-tree.co.uk Essential reading for anyone eager to join the 'community' of family historians and to keep up to date with new developments.

The National Association of Writers' Groups (NAWG) is an organisation that benefits individual writers as well as writers' groups. For a modest annual subscription, individuals can become Associate Members which entitles them to free copies of the NAWG journal *Link.* A friendly no-nonsense organisation that welcomes and encourages writers of all abilities. NAWG, 40 Burstall Hill, Bridlington, East Yorkshire, YO16 7GA, United Kingdom. www.nawg.co.uk

USEFUL ADDRESSES

ISBN Agency, 3rd Floor, Midas House, 62 Goldsworth Road, Woking, Surrey, GU21 6LQ, United Kingdom. Tel: 0870 777 8712   Fax: 0870 777 8714

Nielsen BookData, 89-95 Queensway, Stevenage, SG1 1EA, United Kingdom

Legal Deposit Office, The British Library, Boston Spa, Wetherby, LS23 7BY, United Kingdom. Tel: 01937 546268 Fax: 01937 546273 www.bl.uk

or Irish Copyright Agency, c/o Trinity College Library, College Street, Dublin 2, Eire. Tel: 01 608 1021 Fax: 01 671 9003 www.tcd.ie/library

Copyright Libraries Agency, 100 Euston Street, London, NW1 2HQ, United Kingdom. Tel: 020 7388 5061 Fax: 020 7383 3540 www.cla.ac.uk

Public Lending Right, Richard House, Sorbonne Close, Stockton-on-Tees, TS17 6DA, United Kingdom. Tel: 01642 604699 Fax: 01642 615641 www.plr.uk.com

ACKNOWLEDGEMENTS

The author would like to thank Steve Rudd for reading chapter 10 in draft form and for patiently offering advice on IT matters. Phillip Rendell was a mine of information about the book trade and cheerfully undertook a range of 'odd jobs'.

Very special thanks to Denys Gaskell of Tansley who interrupted a busy schedule to read the entire book in draft and give me his opinion. I am profoundly grateful for his friendly encouragement and good sense.

As always, the author bears responsibility for any remaining mistakes.